Issues in People Management

Workplace Learning,
Culture and Performance

Elliot Stern

Elizabeth Sommerlad

INSTITUTE OF PERSONNEL
AND DEVELOPMENT

IFTDO

© Institute of Personnel and Development 1999

First published 1999

Typeset by Paperweight

Printed in Great Britain by
The Cromwell Press, Trowbridge, Wiltshire

British Library Cataloguing in Publication Data
A catalogue record for this book is available from the British Library

ISBN 0 85292 805 X

INSTITUTE OF PERSONNEL
AND DEVELOPMENT

IPD House, Camp Road, London SW19 4UX
Tel: 0181 971 9000   Fax: 0181 263 3333
Registered Charity No. 1038333.
A company limited by guarantee. Registered in England No. 2931892.
Registered office as above.

Issues in People Management

Workplace Learning,
Culture and Performance

Elliot Stern

Elizabeth Sommerlad

Other titles in the Issues series:

The Changing Role of the Trainer

Employee Motivation and the Psychological Contract

Employment Attitudes in Britain

Fairness at Work and the Psychological Contract

The Impact of People Management Practices on Business Performance

Knowledge Management: A literature review

Managing Learning for Added Value

Performance Management through Capability

The State of the Psychological Contract in Employment

Working to Learn: A work-based route to learning for young people

These titles can be ordered from Plymbridge Distributors
Tel: 01752 202301

The Institute of Personnel and Development is the leading publisher
of books and reports for personnel and training professionals, students,
and all those concerned with the effective management and
development of people at work. For full details of all our titles please
contact the Publishing Department:
tel. 0181-263 3387
fax 0181-263 3850
e-mail publish@ipd.co.uk
The catalogue of all IPD titles can be viewed on the IPD website:
www.ipd.co.uk

- Contents -

Acknowledgements

This report was commissioned by the Institute of Personnel and Development (IPD) from the Evaluation Development and Review Unit (EDRU) of The Tavistock Institute. It is intended to support the IPD in its own policy development and dissemination tasks. The Tavistock Institute welcomes the opportunity to review and synthesise a broad range of research in ways that could be useful to practitioners and managers. The report was prepared by Dr Elizabeth Sommerlad and Elliot Stern with inputs and advice from Jeroen Onstenk of SCO-Kohnstamm Instituut of the University of Amsterdam.

This report draws on a considerable body of research and evaluation work that has been conducted by the Tavistock Institute in recent years. This includes a major review of work-based learning sponsored by DGXXII of the European Commission in 1995-6 and a project within the Learning Society Programme of the Economic and Social Research Council, on Continuing Vocational Training: A Comparative Perspective, between 1996 and 1998. The authors have also drawn on other outputs of the Learning Society Programme as appropriate. At the same time they have sought to draw together international experience from more recent reviews of relevant literature and case studies.

The authors wish to acknowledge the support and advice they have received from Professor David Ashton of Leicester University and Mr. John Stevens of the IPD during the preparation of this report.

Further information about EDRU and its work may be obtained by contacting:

The Administrator
Evaluation Development and Review Unit
The Tavistock Institute
30 Tabernacle Street
London
EC2A 4UE

Tel: 0171 417 0407
Fax: 0171 417 0567
e-mail: edru@tavinstitute.org

Foreword

The work of those who are professionally involved in training and development activities has changed enormously in recent years. Across the globe, the importance of training and its contribution to performance improvement has become recognised. The volume of training and the number of people involved as trainers have increased. But quite apart from the increase in volume, the nature of training has been evolving as this has reflected changes in markets and the development of new organisational structures, management theories and work methods.

Training and development has at its heart the concept of performance improvement. It is based on the belief that people are more effective if they understand what they are doing, have a firm grasp on the theories that underpin their activities and if they aim for continuous improvement in techniques, knowledge and performance informed by a clear view of what constitutes good practice.

Increasingly, benchmarks in training and development effectiveness are being set internationally. In 1998, for the first time, an international organisation, the International Labour Organisation, reviewed the training systems in use in many of the major economies across the globe and drew attention to their differences and the opportunities countries have for learning from each other (ILO World Employment Report, 1998). This work was carried out while the International Federation of Training and Development Organisations was looking to develop a greater understanding of the links between training and competitiveness.

The Institute of Personnel and Development, based in the UK and Ireland, is affiliated to the IFTDO and has in this capacity commissioned the review of academic literature that follows. The Tavistock Institute, based in London, has examined English language research evidence of differences in approaches to workplace learning, learning culture and performance. Although much of the work is UK-based, trouble has been taken to look more widely within Europe, across to the Pacific Rim countries and to a small extent to the Americas. As far as we know, this too is the first study of its type.

The report's contribution

The report sets the development of workplace learning in the context of changing market conditions. It describes a spectrum of organisations, from users of low-tech, low cost operations requiring undifferentiated contributions from employees to high added value organisations wanting a full contribution from highly skilled workers applying a high degree of initiative in non-standard work situations. The background to the report is a gradual move from the former to the latter as a model for economic development.

It is in this context that skill and knowledge requirements are developing fast and methods and methodologies for workplace development are under scrutiny. Among the lessons that can be drawn from the report are the following:

- National cultures and education systems provide the basis on which employers build once young people have moved into the workplace. The explicit close links between education and employment in countries such as Germany have helped to provide such a springboard. Singapore and the other Pacific-rim economies have emulated this approach, developing specific skills and attitudes in their young people.

- The countries mentioned above, and others including Canada, manage the transition from school to work so that people have a greater acceptance of education as an important activity throughout life. The development of core skills is seen as increasingly important, as is their development in a continuous way through school and subsequently at work.

- Increasingly, education at school will need to go beyond imparting knowledge to develop a questioning, analytical, problem-solving, socially aware approach to thinking processes. Those economies not keeping pace with this change are likely to be at a disadvantage because they will not have a sufficiently sound base for the skills needed by high performance workplaces.

- The report quotes Bengtsson's analysis of trends in corporate skill strategies: from product-driven, slanted towards specific skills, via market-driven, responding to quality drivers and shorter life-cycles requiring multi-skilling and flexibility, to process-driven problem-solving, entrepreneurial and customer-oriented communications skills.

- Responding to this a number of workplace learning approaches are being developed. Many are team-based and employ continuous improvement, job enlargement and enrichment and whole-workforce approaches to education and learning centres.

- The shift towards the use of team skills has resulted in innovations in vocational training and a number of examples are quoted including learning islands, in which task, planning, responsibility and social skills are developed within the work process and the Leittext Method which structures trainer-guided phases of theoretical and practical instruction near to the job. Both these methods were developed in Germany.

- Moving towards high performance working puts considerable responsibility on managers and those cultures in which managers have taken responsibility in this way, including Germany, with its Meister system, and Japan, with its emphasis on work-based learning, have a considerable advantage.

- Beyond this, however, mentoring, coaching, job rotation and trainers as tutors on the job are increasingly used. The focus of learning within the workplace is moving from training and teaching to individual and team learning. The role of key workers as working coaches, able to help and support others becomes important as organisational objectives and customer requirements become more sophisticated. Ultimately, all workers may need to become key workers.

- Self-directed learning 'should not be difficult for employees who already know to set realistic goals for themselves, can deal with the ambiguity involved when learning assignments are not structured for them, can plan activities to reach their goal, and can continually assess their progress and revise their goals' (Watkins and Marsick, 1993).

- The development of what may be a radically different approach to learning within the workplace requires an integrated and similarly sophisticated approach to people management more generally. Practices that encourage workers to think and interact to improve the production process are strongly linked to increased productivity. Of particular importance are practices relating to reward, progression and internal labour markets. Trade unions can be particularly effective supporters of new workplace practices.

- Change has to be undertaken at a manageable pace. It needs to take account of the existing culture and may need to overcome ingrained resistance to change, to information exchange and to rigid or one-sided views of the responsibilities of employers and employees for learning.

- Those countries that have a strong existing workplace learning tradition have a clear advantage in the development of the high performance workplace. However, there is no one country that has all the answers. Those cultures that encourage questioning and analytical skills have certain advantages. Transferring learning methods and methodologies is possible but an underlying message from the study is that organisations and countries need to work with that which is positive within their own culture and find ways to adapt ideas – seeing transfer as a process rather than a mechanical move of a tangible object.

One aspect of this report from the Tavistock Institute gave some cause for concern. The researchers were asked to examine the links between learning, culture and performance improvement. Beyond some strong links, for instance between specific training inputs for newly hired workers that significantly increased their productivity in their first few months, the trail went cold. Organisations attest to the importance and contribution of training and many measure and evaluate results systematically but it is difficult to measure the benefits statistically in comparative studies.

This result could seem surprising, coming at a time when increasing evidence is accumulating that people management practices are the main differentiating factor in organisational performance (see studies by West and Patterson, UK, and Huselid, USA). However, this study has shown that, for sophisticated organisations, training and development needs to be integrated within an envelope of people management systems and culture. If this is right, the economists and statisticians may find it more not less easy to find the evidence they are looking for. Meanwhile, managers will continue, rightly, to look for specific links within their organisations. For them the report provides an insight into the challenges they face if they want to move beyond task management and towards the high performance workplace.

Next Steps

The conclusions from this report have contributed to the IFTDO's response to the ILO World Employment Report 1998. In particular, the IFTDO is discussing with the ILO what could be achieved by going beyond its excellent analysis of differences in training systems to look at some of the 'how' questions. The ILO could provide a real service if it were to take the analysis further, providing a framework for information gathering and debate about the development of workplace learning. Although policy decisions have to be made by individual governments and by organisations, there is much that can be learned by international comparison and collaboration, and the IFTDO has offered its full support for such an initiative.

John Stevens
Director, IFTDO Global Task Force, and Director, Development and Public Policy for the Institute of Personnel and Development

Executive summary

This review summarises some of the main things we know, and do not know, about learning in or near the workplace. It considers some of the contemporary trends towards learning organisations and continuous vocational training in the competitive global environment in which we now live. These trends are illustrated both by research studies and case material drawn from a number of different national and cultural contexts. The evidence of links between business performance and training and learning are also considered.

The main findings and conclusions of the report are as follows:

1   There is widespread interest in workplace learning among employers, researchers and policy makers. The main currents of ideas influencing approaches to workplace learning are drawn from experiential learning, work system design, employee development and open/flexible learning. The scope of workplace learning, traditionally associated with methodologies for on-the-job training, has been extended to embrace on-the-job learning. In this newer understanding, learning is part of the process of production and integral to the way in which work is organised. 'Continuous learning work' captures this idea.

2   Much of the research activity in workplace learning is ideas-driven rather than empirically driven. Like the organisational learning literature, it is very substantially normative and prescriptive within the framework of the new techno-economic paradigm. This situation is changing, however, and some serious empirical studies have recently been undertaken which have added considerably to our knowledge of this field.

3   We do not have a good picture of how much workplace learning activity is actually going on, or what form it takes. Surveys of employers' training and management practices are one source of data, but they focus primarily on the more planned and structured activities as part of on-the-job training. Because informal training and learning is so intrinsically linked to the day-to-day operation of the company, it virtually defies quantitative measurement. Nor do we have good knowledge about how extensive workplace learning provision is across employee categories. There is some evidence to suggest that the poorly qualified and older employees are missing out on quality workplace learning, not least because the jobs they perform do not have much potential for learning. There are, however, examples in various EU countries of whole-company strategies aimed at an inclusive approach to workplace learning for all employees.

4   The richest source of data about workplace learning practices is case studies. These are most valuable when they have a comparative element across different sectors and/or organisations, making it possible to generalise, even if in only a limited way. The findings broadly suggest that companies tend to take one of three approaches to workplace learning:

    •   *an incidental learning* approach, where there is little formal investment in on-the-job training beyond what takes place through informal, unplanned learning on the job. These companies tend to perceive their environment as stable, relying on processes and practices that have existed for a long time. To the extent that these companies are operating in markets where competitiveness is determined by other factors such as low cost, it is rational not to train except in the most narrow terms.

- An *event-triggered training* approach where, in addition to incidental learning, formal training or planned, structured on-the-job training is undertaken, but only in response to specific triggers. The most common examples of these triggers are the introduction of new technology or new equipment, some type of workplace reorganisation, staff turnover or external regulatory requirements.

- *Learning organisations* see continuous learning as an integral part of the workplace and, indeed, business strategy. The commitment to training might be quite formalised (eg training needs analysis, career development planning, benchmarking). But emphasis is also placed on creating a stimulating environment where self-directed learning and interaction among colleagues is encouraged. While these organisations often have a formal framework for training, it is very difficult actually to identify training because of the way in which learning is integral to the culture. The consistent factor between companies taking this approach is a strongly held commitment by senior managers to the long-run competitive benefits of investing in people.

Other findings to emerge from recent empirical studies of this kind are that:

- the workplace learning practices of companies often lag behind a commitment to the philosophy of a 'learning organisation', even among those companies reputed to be 'leading edge' in their human resource development strategies

- many factors inhibit effective workplace learning, not all of them amenable to good management practice

- those responsible for introducing new forms of working/learning often have insufficient regard for the micro-politics of the workplace.

5   Despite the very considerable research activity, very few studies address what has actually been learned. Unlike training, which has specified learning outcomes, a curriculum and pedagogy, a great deal of workplace learning is open-ended and ill-specified. Recent UK studies suggest that most learning in the workplace arises naturally out of the demands and challenges of work – solving problems, improving quality and/or productivity, or coping with change – and out of social interactions in the workplace with colleagues, customers or clients. Learning in this way can be either facilitated or constrained firstly by the organisation and allocation of work and secondly the social climate of the work environment.

Companies that seek to instil in their employees, as a whole, a positive attitude towards learning and a desire to learn, ascribe importance to the role of manager as a facilitator of learning. In emphasising process rather than outcome, attention has switched from concern with productivity and appraisal to the creation of a 'learning culture', designed to groom a well-motivated workforce and to prepare workers for coping with change as an ongoing feature of working life. Research points both to the personality, interpersonal skills, knowledge and learning orientation of the manager as a key factor affecting a person's learning at work, as well as to the embeddedness of this role in wider organisational and institutional arrangements.

6   Establishing the linkage between workplace learning and performance improvement is hazardous. Surveys that seek to establish a relationship between employers' training practices and productivity tend to capture the 'hard end' of on-the-job and formal training, and not the more qualitative effects associated with on-the-job learning as a continuous and fluid process.

Case studies offer more scope for considering the linkages, although generalisation is limited. Research is now pointing to the importance of measuring the development of expertise through learning at work, rather than threshold skills/competences. Such expertise is often the combined result of learning and high-performance work practices, however, and it is thus difficult to disentangle effects.

Other recent research suggests that it is not so much the learning processes themselves that give rise to competence development and performance improvement or the way in which they are implemented. These findings direct attention to employee participation, new workplace practices such as incentive-based compensation, and social partner involvement in joint decision-making. In sum, practices that encourage workers to think and interact to improve the production process are strongly linked to increased productivity.

Decisions about whether or not to invest in workplace learning, or to substitute on-the-job training and on-the-job learning for formal off-the-job training involve complex cost-benefit analysis. The economics of instruction-led training has been a difficult challenge but the issues are far more complex for experience-led learning processes and activities. Some initial work has been done in this area, but more is needed.

7   The nature of workplace learning and its effectiveness as an approach to skills development is shaped by the national learning culture. A substantial body of comparative research has pointed to significant national differences in the importance attached to learning as a continuing activity, in the institutional arrangements that support training and learning, and in the way in which training and learning is managed at the enterprise level. Japan and Germany are frequently singled out as examples of countries where the 'learning patrimony' is strongly supportive of workplace learning, although there are differences of opinion about the relative importance of cultural and organisational (institutional) factors.

A recognition of different national learning cultures and contexts is important, not only for understanding what factors provide the important underpinning for effective workplace learning, but also for weighing up the potential for transferring good learning and training practice from one context to another.

It is evident from the empirical research in this field that certain methodologies, such as on-the-job training or the 'key worker'/Meister concept, are highly contextualised. They work well where they have a close fit with underlying values and institutional frameworks. Their embedded nature is such that transfer to a new setting calls for a sophisticated adaptation process. Other training concepts, tools and practices are more generic in nature. These are more readily transplanted to a new organisational setting. Successful transfer is dependent on: a) the degree of symmetry between the host and receiving settings, b) the nature of the object of transfer itself, ie its contextualised/decontextualised nature, and c) the process of adaptation and the actors involved. There is a positive relationship between transferability and homogeneity, longevity, similarity in goals and complementarity in market position.

8 Overall, it would appear that while there is an apparent broad consensus on the value and importance of workplace learning, the adoption and take-up of these ideas and their translation into effective workplace learning strategies and practices is less forthcoming The review of the research literature suggests the four main explanations for this disjunction are as follows:

- The evidence for linkage between productivity and business success is less clear-cut than is sometimes suggested and employers are not willing to make the investment.

- There is a lack of national training and related enterprise policies that can set a context which encourages the emergence of training cultures, especially among those enterprises without a strong training and learning tradition.

- It is sometimes rational for companies tied in to a low-skilled equilibrium not to train except in the most narrow terms.

- A commitment to learning at work is as much a statement of values, an assertion of the kind of society that people want to live in, as an economic imperative. It implies a preference for a more inclusive society.

Chapter 1

The nature of workplace learning

A new and fashionable concept

Workplace learning has become fashionable. Although not a new concept, it has acquired visibility and saliency in contemporary times which has placed it more firmly on the agenda of employers, policy makers and researchers. The reasons for this are many and varied, but owe most to changes brought about by globalisation and new information technologies – what some have called the new 'techno-economic paradigm'. The same pressures lie behind the renewal of interest in 'lifelong learning' and the 'learning organisation'.

Workplace learning sits at the juncture of new thinking concerning the nature of learning about new forms of knowledge, about the transformation of the nature of work and about the modern enterprise in a globalised economy. Literature is found within the areas of education and training, labour market studies, industrial relations, management and business, economics and politics, sociology, anthropology and psychology, policy studies and many others. Those researching and writing in the field view the topic from many different perspectives, bringing their own orientations, methodologies and concerns to discussion of the issues. All this makes for a rich but confusing field of inquiry. This situation is not helped by the fact that those favouring one paradigm frequently use different terminology to describe what is essentially the same phenomenon, or more confusing still, employ the same terminology when they actually mean something different (Candy and Matthews, 1998).

Different meanings of 'workplace learning'

'Workplace learning' has, for these reasons, acquired many different meanings. This elasticity of the term makes it difficult to establish how far there has been a significant shift in human resource development practice towards making more effective use of the workplace as a source of learning. Is there more of it, or a shift in the balance between different kinds of learning at work, or simply a labelling or re-packaging of learning which has always gone on but has not been recognised in the past? Tacit and informal learning, for example, have become *de rigueur* for learning and management theorists, giving rise to instruments or tools designed to capture it. But it is also possible that the same activity might one year be seen as simply being told what to do, and the next year come to be regarded as a form of job-related training (Mayhew and Keep, 1996). In somewhat similar vein, concepts such as the 'quality of working life', which have been in currency for some decades, have been brought in under the umbrella of workplace learning. We thus cannot be sure to what extent we are looking at a new phenomenon or at an ideological shift which has given workplace learning a new prominence.

One way of categorising the different understandings of workplace learning is based on the degree of separation between learning and work:

- the workplace as a site for learning

- the workplace as a learning environment

- learning and working as inextricably linked.

In the first, learning and working are spatially separated, with some form of structured learning activity occurring off or near the job. This can take a variety of forms. Most commonly, it takes the form of in-company training which may be offered in a company training centre, an open-learning centre or near to the job. Much of the training activity taking place away from the job makes extensive use of the workplace as a source of experiential learning, with instructional practices increasingly aimed at linking skills development with the business objectives of the enterprise. New modes of learning include use of IT simulations and other 'experimental' or laboratory type experiences. Innovations, such as 'learning islands' which are found in Germany, are located on the shop floor and mirror the production process while primarily having a training function for apprentices and trainees. The role of trainer as staff developer is uppermost in this approach.

In the second approach, the workplace itself becomes an environment for learning. The main focus here is on a diverse array of on-the-job training activities, ranging across a spectrum from the highly structured to those with minimal educational intervention. Learning is, however, intentional and planned, aimed at training employees by supporting, structuring and monitoring their learning. Two main forms of on-the-job training can be distinguished:

- the structuring of experience-led learning opportunities in the workplace through such means as job rotation, sequencing of the learner's activities, increasing the variety and complexity of work tasks

- training on the job through coaching, mentoring, work shadowing, supervision and job instruction.

The role of manager as staff developer is highlighted in this approach, conceived in terms of appraisal and target setting, and planned development opportunities. While the range of methods for supporting learning has widened, the underpinning concept is based on learning goals being clearly specified and learning opportunities being planned. Mechanisms for supporting learning include learning plans, individual professional development plans, journal diaries, and review sessions. In some countries, specific methodologies such as Leittext have been introduced to support the reflective process and provide a stronger basis for the transfer of learning to different settings.

The third form of learning has recently come to be known as continuous learning work. Zuboff (1988) captures the essence of this kind of learning in her oft-quoted comment:

> The behaviours that define learning and the behaviours that define being productive are one and the same. Learning is not something that requires time out from being engaged in productive activity: learning is the heart of productive activity. To put it simply, learning is the new form of labour.

In this view, learning becomes an everyday part of the job and is built into routine tasks. Employees are expected to learn not only the skills related to their own jobs, but also the skills of others in their work unit and how their work unit relates to the operation and goals of the business. Furthermore, employees are expected to teach, as well as learn from, their co-workers. In short, the entire work environment is geared towards and supports the learning of new skills, knowledge and understanding (Watkins and Marsick, 1993). Learning is viewed not as ancillary to, but effectively as inseparable from, the productive role. Newer forms of work organisation, notably those described as 'high performance' or 'high skills' are designed to obtain the full benefits of a more competent and responsible workforce; for example, decentralised authority, self-managed teams, and total quality management (Finegold and Levine, 1997).

There is also an emphasis in this third approach on learning that arises out of the problems, puzzles and challenges of work itself. Workers develop skills, knowledge and understanding through dealing with the challenges posed by their work – improving productivity and/or quality, getting things done, coping with change, solving problems – and out of social interactions in the workplace with colleagues and customers/clients. This kind of informal learning is either facilitated or constrained first by the organisation and allocation of work and second by the social climate of the work environment (Eraut et al, 1998). There is a view that most people do not take sufficient advantage of those learning opportunities which do present themselves. Strategies aimed at remedying this situation include both developing people's capability to recognise and seek out learning opportunities and engage in self-directed learning, and also enhancing organisational understanding of the learning process and how it might best be supported.

The merits of a continuous learning work environment have been promoted by writers on learning organisations. For one group of writers, emphasis is placed on strategies for strengthening informal learning in the workplace through, for example, equipping managers with the skills to support the learning of their subordinates, linking formal and informal learning through better planning, and creating a stimulating environment where self-directed learning and interaction among colleagues is encouraged. For another group, the prime focus is on organisational dialogue in a collective setting that results in mutual learning upon which the organisation can act (Dixon, 1994). Here we see emphasis on quality circles, action learning, continuous improvement teams and other kinds of communication mechanisms that foster and support vertical and horizontal communication.

The nature of learning and knowledge

Behind these approaches to workplace learning lie different understandings about the nature of learning and knowledge. Current training models, such as those prevailing in off-the-job learning centres and company training centres, emphasise job-related knowledge and skills as if it is possible to divorce them from the rest of the worker's life. Informed by behaviourist and cognitive theories, their task is defined primarily in terms of increasing the individual's knowledge and skills.

On-the-job training and learning, as in the second approach above, recognises that, for learning to be effective, one must consider the context in which job skills are embedded. The social unit that shapes the individual's actions at work is above all the organisation and the immediate work group. To the extent that it also fosters self-reflective learning, it raises questions about the individual's perception of him/herself in relation to the job and organisation. This broader context not only determines what kinds of skills and competencies are required for effective performance of the individual worker and the organisation as a whole, but it also provides the enabling (or disabling) conditions for learning. It draws on functionalist and contextual theories which emphasise situatedness and interaction.

In the third approach, learning is seen more in social and collective than in individual terms. It is about participation in 'communities of practice' or social aggregates such as teams, cross-functional groups, and even the communities with which the organisation interacts. Learning here means more than the acquisition of skills, but refers to a variety of processes, including:

> a broadening of the instrumental focus of learning, integration of personal and job-related development, an organisational model that functions as a learning system, a focus on group as well as individual learning, a concern for critical reflectivity and for problem setting as well as problem solving, emphasis on informal learning and development of the organisation as a learning environment.
>
> (Marsick, 1987).

Acquiring competencies and skills is almost secondary with respect to these processes of constructing new social identities and ways of thinking. The emphasis given to sense-making, system-thinking, social and communication skills and team-based problem solving underline the social nature of learning. Moreover, there is recognition that people can acquire knowledge and skills informally, quite independently of conscious attempts to learn. There is renewed interest here in learning theories in which the human person is depicted as a truly social being, and learning is viewed as a social activity.

Accommodating a social model of learning

The confusion that exists around workplace learning is attributable in large part to the shift in paradigmatic thinking which has not yet been fully grasped. The individualistic orientation is so strongly grounded in the training model as well as in learning theory, that researchers, policy makers and human resource developers alike have been slow to realise that the new organisation forms call for new social models of learning which stress the collective rather than the individual perspective.

This discussion on workplace learning has bypassed issues to do with humanising the workplace or empowering the workers. For many people, however, the allure of workplace learning lies more in the prospect it holds out for personal development than in its more instrumental purposes. It is noteworthy that a small critical literature is beginning to develop analysing the fissures between workplace learning's promise of enhanced equality and democracy, its promise of 'empowerment for stakeholders', and its reality as an agenda of powerholders interested in a more vibrant capitalism (McIlroy, 1997; Hart, 1993).

Chapter 2

Workplace learning for a new economy

Chapter overview

- There is a widely shared consensus about macro-level changes in society, propelled in the main by new technology and global competitiveness, that they are driving the take-up and introduction of new product strategies and new forms of work organisation, and are setting up a demand for broader and deeper skills in an enlarged proportion of the workforce.

- Much of the policy and research literature is framed by this vision, popularised as 'post-industrial' or 'post-Fordist' society. It has a deterministic flavour, with prescriptive solutions for how Britain might best respond to the new hypercompetitive environment. A dominant theme is the call for the adoption of competitive strategies based on high quality production and high value added and a more flexible, autonomous and high-skilled workforce.

- Such a visionary view obscures a reality that is revealed in a much more piecemeal and contradictory fashion from empirical studies. Employers do not all experience similar pressures for work reorganisation or changing skill requirements. For some firms, a rational response is to continue with a low skills strategy, and to maintain training at minimal stable levels. Moreover, it would seem that the pressures for workplace training are as likely to come from government regulatory requirements as from new production processes or ideas of the 'learning organisation'. We therefore need to take a much differentiated, and some might say sceptical, view of macro-level changes and the way these are impinging on firms.

- Getting an accurate picture of company training policy and practice is difficult. Some of the observable trends would appear to be counter-intuitive. Most broad-brush surveys of employers' training practices are concerned with training that is pedagogically structured in some way, but the newer kinds of workplace learning stress experience-based modes of learning which tend to be integrated into production processes and the way work is organised. Learning of this kind is difficult to define, capture and record, especially with survey instruments. We are mostly in the dark about the nature and extent of this kind of non-formal or informal learning.

- Case studies of companies with innovative training policies and practices are suggestive of emergent trends in workplace learning. Even so, it would appear that very few companies conform to the Human Resource Management textbook model of the progressive 'learning organisation'.

- Drawing together the data from multiple sources, we can begin to get a picture of changing practices among employers in using the workplace as a site for, as well as a source of, learning. Overall, there is indeed an increasing emphasis on more planned and structured learning in the workplace in place of off-the-job training and incidental 'sitting by Nellie' modes of learning. But clearly there is a long way to go in realising the full potential of the workplace as a learning environment.

The macro-context

Globalisation, technology and markets

Contemporary interest in workplace learning is generally explained in relation to wider trends in Western industrial societies. Increasing economic globalisation and interdependence, together with the mobility of capital, have caused whole industries to shrink or expand, shifting the demand for skills and the availability of job opportunities for particular communities and whole nations.

The increasing sophistication of technology has been a powerful aid to this process, in terms of telecommunications, transport, IT and many other features of economic life. New manufacturing technology, especially information technology such as computer-aided design, just-in-time production, optimised production technology, and rapid response systems have brought in their wake considerable changes to production processes, which have been mirrored by changes in the organisation of human capital.

In employment, change is evident in the introduction of new organisational structures and work practices, in the reduced size of workplaces, and in the design, production and delivery of new products and services. Much routine work has been automated, with diminishing opportunities for unskilled and semi-skilled employment (Fryer, 1997).

The search for new management and organisational paradigms is also being fuelled by market drivers such as more demanding and sophisticated customers (Starkey, 1996). Quality is privileged over price. Mass production is giving way to flexible production, demanding in turn an increased knowledge base among employees and a capability for ongoing learning. Emphasis is placed on such personal attributes as confidence, attitudes, motivation, and pride in the work, with attention to quality and customer care.

In all, the changes add up to what such popularisers as Toffler, Handy and Drucker have termed 'post-industrial society'. Prescriptive solutions for dealing with the demands of the new techno-economic order, put forward by policy makers, researchers and political parties, have largely centred on two linked strategies – moving towards a higher value-added strategy and a higher-skills workforce. In the UK, this represents a significant shift away from the 'low skills equilibrium' (Finegold and Soskice, 1988) which has characterised industrial policy and employer behaviour hitherto. In a high skills equilibrium, enterprises have to become more flexible, add more value to their products and services and consider the human capacities within the organisation as a competitive resource. Such a shift in strategy requires continuous lifelong skills formation, development and improvement (Onstenk, 1993; Drake, 1995).

Assumptions of this kind are reflected in the macro-economic models of labour market developments, such as those undertaken by the Institute of Manpower

Studies and the Institute of Employment Research (Booth and Snower, 1996) as well as in the policy prescriptions of OECD (Bengtsson, 1993) and the Commission on Workforce Quality and Labour Market Efficiency in the United States (Shackleton et al, 1995). In a detailed examination of the arguments for the increased emphasis on training in the political agendas of the leading industrial nations, Shackleton et.al noted a common view that 'the quality of the workforce seems to be all a country has going for it if it wishes to maintain and improve its living standards in to the next century'.

Continuous improvement

There is an apparent consensus that if firms want to stay in business they will need to invest in continuous human resource development (Ashton, Green and Lowe, 1993). Booth and Snower (1996) sum up a widely held belief about the nature of the new work environment:

> The forces of technological change and trade have transformed the labour market, continually changing the nature of jobs and raising the rate at which skills become obsolete. Employers are demanding more than a well-defined stable set of skills; they are demanding adaptability, the ability to adapt one's skills to ever changing circumstances. And there is no easy way for workers to become adaptable in this sense, other than going through a continual process of training and retraining.

Underpinned by human capital theory, the dominant theme in much of the literature is that only when knowledge and skills are constantly updated and upgraded will nations, organisations and individuals be able to survive and prosper in this post-Fordist, post-modern era.

The firm and market: not the state

The enterprise is increasingly seen as a source of learning for a large proportion of the working population. Policy makers have increasingly been relying on the market to address labour market issues, including skill formation. New attention is being paid to continuous vocational training (CVT) alongside initial training. At the same time, new forms of 'teamwork', 'integrated work systems' and 'learning organisations' are being proposed as aspects of work organisation that makes work-based learning more possible (Brown and Duguid, 1991; Jones and Hendry, 1994).

In the UK, within the parameters of the commitment to a 'free training market', various enabling initiatives have been taken at a national policy level to support movement towards a higher skills equilibrium. These include the creation of a framework for National Vocational Qualifications, the endorsement and introduction of National Education and Training Targets aimed at improving the UK's international competitiveness, the setting up of the Investors in People programme, and the issue of White Papers such as the recent one on lifelong learning – all of which legitimise a general discourse on the need for a higher skilled workforce.

Scanning the research literature in relevant fields of enquiry, one gains the impression of a wholesale transformation of the work and occupational structure. There is a prescriptive quality about much of the writing, drawing either on selected case studies of 'leading' or best-practice firms, or on normative models of the 'firm of the future'. It is often difficult to disentangle the empirical from the rhetorical. The preoccupation with post-Fordism, human resource management and lifelong learning – and some of the broad sweep visionary literature utilised – is, however, in danger of obscuring the unprepossessing features of the workplace in many industry sectors, and a realistic measure of its potential, or lack of it, as a site for educational development.

Recently, we have begun to see a more measured assessment of workplace reform and the appropriate role of workplace learning (Tavistock Institute, 1998a; Onstenk, 1997b; Keep and Mayhew, 1997), and a developing critique of post-industrial society and its potential for an increasingly polarised labour market. Research has revealed a growing disparity between the skills and working conditions of professional, managerial and technical jobs on the one hand, and those of the growing peripheral forms of employment on the other (Ashton, Maguire and Spilsbury, 1990; Brown and Scase, 1991).

Working with companies in the Netherlands, Onstenk (1997b) has looked critically at what is involved in team working and 'continuous improvement' – a byword for progressive workplaces. In companies where lean production prevails, it appears that learning in the group is restricted to learning a series of low-level short cycles just by mere repetition. And although continuous improvement is actively pursued, there is no real rise in skill level, but rather a broadening of the available range of low-level skills which enhances the flexibility of production and usability of labour power, but not the level of competence (or the market value) of the employee. The quality of on-the-job learning depends on the sequence of problems and 'critical events' occurring in day-to-day work practice. So differences in design and organisational choice in the same job and work process can have large consequences for learning opportunities.

The low skill alternative

Keep and Mayhew (1997) point to countervailing developments in the UK work structure. On the one hand there are trends towards a higher global requirement for skills within the British economy. Companies such as British Steel, Rover Group and ICI are outstanding examples where competitive strategies based on high quality production and high added value mean that a more flexible, autonomous and highly skilled workforce is an essential prerequisite for success. On the other hand, there are large areas of employment where skill requirements and training efforts are, and will remain, limited and where there may be active deskilling of segments of the workforce. Employers pursuing product market strategies based on the production of low-quality, low-cost goods and services using Taylorist methods of work organisation are more likely to want a cheap, relatively low-skilled workforce of people who do what they are told.

Utilisation of competitive strategies based on price rather than quality provides an important role in determining employers' perceptions of the levels of skill they require. As Keep and Mayhew (1997) observe, the case for up-skilling and high value-added strategies may also be undermined by the structure of demand in the UK economy. Producing high-tech, high-quality goods and services that require high levels of skills is not, in itself, intrinsically important to a company. The issue of overriding concern is whether or not its product market strategy allows it to survive and to make adequate levels of profit. If companies can achieve these ends through the production of low-cost, low-quality, high-volume goods and services that require minimal skill levels, then there is little reason for them to alter their strategies.

If the structure and organisation of work in a particular organisation is not undergoing change, then 'more training' as a generalised prescription may make little sense. Training demands may be essentially predictable and readily met by existing provision, and incremental personnel development may be sufficient to meet any new skills demands. Moreover, adding value to products and upskilling the workforce is not the only competitive strategy available to firms. Growth via take-over, and cost minimisation are just two of a wide range of alternatives.

Organisational choice, shaped by actors

Researchers at the Tavistock Institute (1998b) take issue with the largely deterministic stance that pervades much of the literature. Work organisation and skills are not, they assert, determined in a linear fashion by particular technological and market conditions. Options are available and strategic choices can be made. In their research in companies, they observed such options at the level of the enterprise as: to professionalise or routinise work; to out-source and subcontract or to integrate functions internally; to invest in IT and people of IT instead of people; to centralise or decentralise control; to introduce teams and reduce hierarchy – or not; and to go for mass markets or flexible specialisation. Such choices are not the prerogative of management, but are in fact influenced by a wider set of players – including social partners, regional bodies, training institutions – and expressed through labour markets, national education and training systems and various resources for innovation within which firms are embedded.

There are differing views about the nature and pace of change towards post-Fordist models of work organisation, and the extent to which all firms in the longer term will need to shift towards a high value-added, high skills strategy. Sectoral differences are important here, and these are examined in more detail in the next chapter. It does, however, seem that the capacity and possibility for a critical number of enterprises in a given country to change towards a post-Tayloristic and more efficient work organisation is strongly influenced by the way that country's education and labour market institutions operate (Bengtsson, 1993).

Pressures at the enterprise level for workplace learning

Within a market-led training system, such as is found in the UK, the level of employee training is driven primarily by employers' perceptions about whether or not it is their business interest to train. This voluntarist tradition has in the past resulted in low levels of training relative to European counterparts in different industry sectors. Pressures stemming from the macro-changes in the competitive environment discussed above, together with policy-enabling frameworks and incentives, are thought likely to be making an impact on employers' attitudes and practices towards the need for continuing vocational training and workplace learning. The discourse of management theorists around the concept of the learning organisation, as well as policy pronouncements on lifelong learning, also help to create a more receptive climate for human resource development and the general upskilling of the workforce. These ideas are also likely to influence workers, and

LIVERPOOL JOHN MOORES UNIVERSITY
LEARNING SERVICES

possibly also to create employee demand for qualifications as well as professional development and learning opportunities at work.

Empirical studies, based on a diverse set of enterprises in different industry sectors, paint a broadly consistent picture of the important influences on companies' decisions to invest in training on a continuing basis. The dominant pattern in workplace training running across different industries corresponds to what Felstead and Green (1996) term 'training floors', meaning basic training needs that could not be set aside even under the axe of a severe cost-cutting management. Training provision of this kind is predominantly reactive, propelled mainly by legislative and safety needs, and indeed, customer demands. A second main influence on training activity relates to the competitive strategy of companies, although here the findings vary between sectors and are sometimes counter-intuitive. Other influences on training reflect the nature of companies as 'open systems', where ideas and ideals, incentives and rewards in the wider environment can shape company policies and training practices. There is more scope here for a proactive approach to training, where the long-term goal involves instilling in employees, as a whole, a positive attitude towards learning and a desire to learn.

Regulatory requirements

The findings from a diverse set of studies show that pre-eminent among the demands on employers for training are the requirements for compliance with standards in regulatory areas. In a number of industries, regulations are in force to minimise dangers to workers and customers, such as the Food Safety Act, the Control of Substances Hazardous to Health Regulations, the Financial Services Act, the New Roads and Street Works Act and the Construction Regulations. These impose legal obligations on firms to demonstrate that staff have received sufficient training to work competently and safely. In some cases, the regulatory requirement extends to certified training for supervisors of such works.

Several empirical studies, in industries as diverse as health, financial services, construction, hotel and catering and manufacturing, report findings from employers that legal and regulatory requirements were their primary reason for initiating work-based training (Scott and Cockrill, 1997; Raper et al 1997, Felstead and Green, 1996 , and Tavistock Institute, 1998a). Such regulatory innovation, ironically, has often arisen as a response to deregulation. It seems that contrary to the 'free training market' rhetoric, the State is using elements of training to address gaps and/or inefficiencies resulting from market deregulation (Tavistock Institute, 1998a).

Further externally imposed obligations arise from occupation labour markets. To remain members of their respective professional bodies, qualified individuals are required to keep their qualifications up to date by accumulating a set number of points during the years. Non-professionals, too, may have to demonstrate their continued occupational competence. Felstead and Green's (1996) research suggests that diverse government and professional regulations serve to 'harden up' otherwise soft budgets and prevent training expenditures being cut, even with the extensive pressures of the recession.

Quality standards

A second pressure on employers to provide workplace training is linked to the adoption of BS5750 and ISO9002 quality assurance standards and associated quality audits. Behind this presenting rationale typically lay a competitive strategy based on the production of quality products and/or the delivery of a quality service. Scott and Cockrill (1997) found that among small and medium enterprises (SMEs) in the construction industry, quality assurance procedures associated with ISO9002 had percolated into almost a third of the companies surveyed, with another three firms currently pursuing the standard, and this had forced a greater formalisation and intensification of training activity in those firms adopting it. Case study findings here are strongly supported by data from the Employers' Manpower and Skills Practices Survey (EMPS) based on a representative survey of around 1,700 employers. As reported by Raper et al (1997), the strongest motivator was the desire to improve quality standards in the face of competition. Pressure of this kind may be exerted by individual customers demanding a better quality of service, as in the retail trade, or it may come through a business organisation's insistence that a supplier has quality standards in place.

Supply-chain factors

The importance of quality as a driver of workplace training was felt in other ways as well. In Felstead and Green's (1996) study of more than 200 managers of companies that were undertaking work-related training, a number were suppliers to large companies including Marks and Spencer, Ford, Boots and Rover which enforced their own quality standards, requiring training of the workforce. Many Japanese companies in the UK similarly emphasise suppliers' training systems, as part of an extended keiretsu. A similar finding emerged from the Tavistock Institute (1998a) study of companies, whereby component suppliers were required to train as part of their subcontracting arrangements. None of these forms of regulation are statutory, but taken together with the intensification of competition they have acquired their own force.

Being part of a supplier chain influences training decisions in other ways. Not all the best training practices emanate outwards from the core company. The use of contractors brings into a company different forms of practice, which both provides examples of alternative training practice and can suggest the need to harmonise skills and competences across sub-contractors and between sub-contractors and 'core' employees (Tavistock Institute, 1998a).

Competitive pressures for customer care and market positioning

It is evident from empirical studies that competitive pressures are a significant source of influence of companies' training policies and practices. Linked with increased competition for product market share is the supremacy of the customer, and the need to develop 'softer' communication skills as part of customer service and selling. In detailed case studies of eight UK companies in four different sectors – banking, textiles, distribution and retail – Raper et al (1997) identified common pressures for training, driven in the main by intensified competition in product markets. At the customer end, changes in product market gave rise to a demand for training of workers for technical knowledge of new products as well as communication and social skills for those at the interface with customers.

Not all training associated with customer care is about new product strategies and winning new market share. Felstead and Green (1996) found that a significant influence on training in this area, induced by the recession, was aimed more at retaining existing customers than on winning new ones. Several managers in their study had introduced customer care programmes entailing an increase in training activity in order to diffuse knowledge of what the company was selling, and of its customer needs.

Even the construction industry is affected by the dominance of the 'customer as king'. Scott and Cottrill (1997) found that in a number of SME firms in their sample, some manual staff training was directed towards fostering a positive customer image at the soft end – driving behaviour, personal appearance, manner and dress of operatives.

Market positioning was also found to be the primary motivator for provision and uptake of training among small and medium enterprises. Based on a survey sample of 2,000 SMEs in the West Midlands, supplemented by in-depth interviews with nearly 250 owner-managers in five occupation sectors, Hyland and Matlay (1997) found that enterprises choosing high technology market niches were compelled by competitive pressures to provide more training opportunities than those operating in more traditional markets.

It might be expected that those companies most exposed to global competitive forces would be at the leading edge in adopting innovative training practices to sustain a competitive position. Paradoxically, Labour Force Survey data reveal that those industries most exposed to international competition recorded training incidence below the industrial average for both 1990 and 1992, while by far the greatest amount of training took place in the non-tradeables sector (containing much of the public sector) that is least exposed to international competition (Greenhalgh and Mavrotas, 1993).

Human resource management

Whereas the above influences are primarily external to the company or a function of market positioning, other influences on training derive mainly from internal (HR) management practices. Sometimes these are linked with external rewards and incentives. The introduction of TQM and other quality improvement processes, requiring employee knowledge of new procedures, as well as the reason for their introduction, was found to be a principal motivator of training in the study by Raper et al (1997). Training is also being driven internally by the introduction of appraisals which serve both to identify training needs and to create a demand for training (Tavistock Institute, 1998a; Raper et al 1997). External awards, in particular Investors in People, because of its links with business performance and Training Enterprise Councils, emerge as another main source of influence on companies, especially in industries with less developed training cultures (Scott and Cockrill, 1997; Tavistock Institute, 1998a).

Links with work organisations

It would seem that there is little evidence of uptake of 'learning organisation' ideas and ideals as a direct stimulus to training activity, although this may reflect the concern of most empirical studies cited here with what might be termed 'hard' rather than 'soft' learning processes.

Workplace reorganisation involving a shift to multi-skilling, team working and delayering did not figure prominently as a trigger for training activity. An exception here was the study by Raper and colleagues (1997), who found that in companies where the restructuring process involved consequent devolution of responsibility for training to line managers and supervisors, then this was commonly an impetus to train employees for their enlarged work role. Brown et al (1994), on the other hand, found in their study of British companies committed to team working that they did not always pick out coaching expertise and training for this role as the way forward. Instead, they used their appraisal systems to encourage team members to learn each other's skills. Scott and Cockrill (1997), citing data from the Association of Direct Labour Organisations, likewise report that despite recent developments towards multiskilling which has occurred as part of more broad-ranging sector-specific attempts to modify traditional occupational demarcations, little or no training is being provided to enable employees to become multiskilled. A similar finding is reported by Walsh, Green and Steedman (1993), whose case study firms had a training policy dedicated to producing more multi-skilled and flexible employees, although in practice the degree of multi-skilling was limited in all but one case. Much of the training effort was devoted to developing more flexible attitudes to work rather than to developing a wider range of higher-level skills.

Product life-cycle influence on training activity

The empirical studies cited above, spanning as they do a cross-section of industries, help to fill what has until now been a major gap in our knowledge of the reasons for training beyond what broad surveys have been able to tell us. What these studies do not reveal, however, is the linkages between the triggers or pressures for certain kinds of training activity and the choices made by employers as to how those training needs are best met. Two studies, adopting a product life-cycle approach, offer a dynamic perspective on the forces or pressures that lie behind a decision at enterprise level to invest in particular combinations of education and training. Although presented as generic models, in both cases the models are empirically derived.

Bengtsson (1993) identifies three phases or stages in the strategy of an enterprise responding to external changes and forces, with each stage having different implications for the skill structure and competences needed.

A first phase is where the stimulus to training relates to some tangible investment by the enterprise, often in terms of new technology or the launching of new products and services. The education and training needs tends in these circumstances to be product specific and when the workforce masters the new equipment and products these investments in education and training flatten out. This phase could be called a product-driven education and training strategy, and its influence on the skill structure is clearly slanted towards specific skills.

A second phase emerges when the enterprise finds itself in a more competitive environment and has to respond to shorter life-cycles of its products and services, as well as to produce both greater variety of products and higher quality. In this phase, enterprises tend to look for a more flexible work organisation, and their investment in education and training increasingly focuses on the need to develop multi-skilled workers capable of performing many different tasks within a flexible rk organisation. Job rotation becomes frequent, and thus so does on-the-job training.

Within this phase, education and training efforts lose the *ad hoc* characteristics of the first phase and become a permanent feature of the business strategy. The kind of skill structure that tends to develop in this phase is, above all, shaped by the multi-skilled worker and the need for competences that reflect the mastering and integration of hitherto isolated and fragmented domains of the enterprise. This is a market-driven education and training strategy of an enterprise, based on the need to respond to quality and shorter life-cycles of products and services.

A third phase tends to emerge particularly in small and knowledge-intensive enterprises, many of which are found in the service sector either as independent enterprises or closely related to the manufacturing industries as business service firms. Increasingly, the raw material with which these enterprises are working is knowledge and information. Their education and training strategy is a dual one, and tends to concentrate on recruitment and on the creation of a positive learning environment at work. In these enterprises, learning and working increasingly become an integrated process. The skill structure that tends to emerge has its priority around problem solving, entrepreneurial and customer-oriented communication skills. This phase could be called the *process-driven strategy for education and training*, where most new tasks have a new knowledge dimension.

As a general trend, Bengtsson discerns that the critical mass of enterprises is now moving from phase one to phase two, and that the fastest employment growth in the services sector, although not in absolute terms, tends to be in enterprises that are in phase three (for instance, business service firms).

In somewhat similar vein, Hendry et al (1991) postulate a dynamic 'skill training cycle' developed on the analogy of the product life cycle which derives from the authors' study of skill needs, training and development in small and medium enterprises. Like Bengtsson, their empirical research suggests that the requirements of SMEs for formal and systematic training and other kinds of workplace learning are geared to the maturity of the firm and the types of skill needed to sustain firm growth. Through an analysis of the different types of skill supply strategies taken by SMEs corresponding to their business strategies, and the maturity of the markets in which they are functioning, their study reveals that firms of different kinds have very clear reasons for favouring particular combinations of young entrant training, *ad hoc* or hands-on or systematic training, management development, general team building and informal learning.

Trends in training and learning in the workplace

Gathering information on training in the workplace is not a simple matter. The informal learning that is attached to any job experience is by its very nature, difficult to document. And even formal training is not easily captured because of a lack of consensus on what should be included and because few employers track these activities systematically. Reviewing empirical studies in Australia, the United States and the United Kingdom, British researchers (Blundell et al, 1995) recently documented an extraordinary range of definitions of training given in surveys. Even within the domain of individual-based surveys in Britain, different measures of training intensity appear. It is also possible that the same activity might one year be seen as simply being told what to do, and the next year come to be regarded as a form of job-related training (Mayhew and Keep, 1996).

This 'messiness' suggests that to get a rounded picture of employer training practices and trends, we need to draw on multiple sources of data – surveys, case studies of workplaces, mappings of innovations in workplace learning – that are framed in both training and learning paradigms. From what we know about the demands of the new economy and the pressures on employers to make more use of the workplace for learning, we might expect to find evidence for:

- greater use of in-company training in preference to external training provision

- a rising proportion of on-the-job to off-the-job training within the company

- a move from planned and structured learning (whether on or off the job) towards informal learning or continuous learning work.

During the 1990s, a body of empirical studies has been built up that takes us a good way towards mapping and understanding these trends. The studies vary in scope, reliability, generalisability and quality. But together they give insights into what is happening in this sphere, and can suggest where further more rigorous research might be called for. Comparative data across the EU and where similar studies have been undertaken, such as Canada and the Netherlands, also help to establish what seems to be a common response to the new economic order.

Trends in workplace learning and training may be evident in a number of areas. We are concerned here with empirical studies which shed light on trends with respect to:

- the amount of training activity and the form that it takes

- the beneficiaries of workplace learning and training.

The extent and nature of training activity

National surveys

What do we know about workforce training and learning in Britain? One source of data is the national Labour Force Survey. The findings show an upswing in employers' training activities but the broad brush nature of the survey does not distinguish between training that is there simply to fulfil a government regulation, and training that is aimed at further skilling of a company's workforce. Both types of training constitute an augmentation of human capital, but the sort of training likely to be relevant to addressing performance improvement will have a longer-term pay-off than that of satisfying immediate regulatory needs (Keep and Mayhew, 1996).

National company training surveys provide a more detailed picture of changes in employers' training practices. Raper et al (1997) cite the findings from a number of such surveys. Selected with an eye to balance between reliability, comprehensiveness and recency of data collection, they include the Employers' Manpower and Skills Practices survey (EMPS, Dench, 1993), the Personnel

Management Plus survey (PMP, Saggers, 1994) and the Industrial Society's Training Trends (ISTT, Industrial Society, 1994). To these may be added the longitudinal surveys undertaken as part of the evaluation of the Investors in People initiative (IIP, Hillage and Moralee, 1996). This study was based on three annual surveys (1993-95) of 1,800 employers involved and not involved with Investors in People, supplemented by case study interviews.

Taken together, the results of these surveys suggest that several changes are taking place in the delivery of training and development at the level of the workplace. The IIP survey confirms national figures for an upward rise in training activities, reflected in an increase in the total amount of off- and on-the-job training among all groups of employers in the longitudinal sample, from an average of 10.9 days in 1993 to 16.4 days in 1995. More revealing is the shift in training strategy. One marked change is a refocusing of in-company training in preference to the use of external courses. According to the PMP survey, 70 per cent of firms had increased their use of in-company training, with 69 per cent saying that they expected to increase it still further over the next couple of years.

Changes in the mode of training delivery are also evident. Several surveys report an increase in the use of on-the-job training. The IIP survey reported a rise in the proportion of training done on the job from just over half in 1993 to almost three-quarters in 1995, while the PMP survey found that 56 per cent of companies had increased their use of OJT. Both EMPS and IIP surveys report an increase in OJT given to manual workers or other non-management employees.

Perhaps most significant of all, companies are devolving responsibility for training and development to line managers. The PMP survey reported that 65 per cent of employers had increased the role of line management in training over the last two years, compared with 5 per cent who had reduced it. The ISTT surveys appear to corroborate this finding. For example, 41 per cent of respondents thought the trend towards the devolution of training budgets was unlikely to be reversed over the next two or three years. Furthermore, 71 per cent felt that line managers welcomed the greater involvement in training which devolution entails.

National surveys of the kind reported above tend to be biased towards large companies, and are therefore likely to give a misleading picture of training practices and trends in the small business sector, which makes up around 95 per cent of all firms in Britain and accounts for approximately 35 per cent of total employment (Dyson, 1990). A study of 2,000 SME owner-managers in the West Midlands (Matlay, 1994, 1996) revealed a yawning gulf between mostly positive attitudes to training and largely insignificant take-up and involvement in training. Around 87 per cent had not provided any training during the 12 months prior to interviews, while a further 7 per cent provided up to one day's training. Workplace training, it would appear, is not a prominent feature of SMEs, notwithstanding the massive investment in this sector by the NCVQ (FEFC, 1994; IES, 1995) which might have been expected to boost on-the-job training.

Company case studies

The broad nature of these surveys masks trends that may be more evident among the leading-edge companies with a commitment to continuous vocational training and learning at work, and which might be expected to set benchmarking standards for other companies. Two studies of such companies have recently been undertaken, adding to our knowledge in this area (Tavistock Institute, 1998a; Raper et al, 1997).

The main findings to emerge from the cross-industry study by Raper et al, which was based on eight companies, were the following.

- Overall, there was indeed an increasing emphasis on the workplace itself as a site and source of learning. Off-the-job training courses were in decline; those that remained were being pared down into truncated versions of their former selves. In their place was some increase in computer-based training and open learning.

- There was also some evidence of 'ownership' of employee development by lower-level line managers and, to some extent, by operatives themselves.

- On-the-job training was emerging in a form that could distinguish it from the traditional, peremptory, 'sitting by Nellie'.

- There were some indications that learning on the job was becoming more structured and systematic. But the application of such techniques seemed to be restricted to a limited number of tasks and to the initial stages of learning required to undertake these roles.

- There were few signs that continual learning beyond the introductory phase – still less to the level of enabling and fostering innovation in methods – was being fostered.

The case studies conducted by the Tavistock Institute (1998a) as part of its ESRC-funded Learning Society research project also found an increase in work-based learning and a reduction in formal courses. Similarly, a more structured approach to learning on the job was indicated by an increased prevalence of on-the-job trainers working with employees in their workplace. Another significant development was the establishment of learning centres in five of the six case study companies, coupled with an increased emphasis on individuals taking responsibility for their own learning. These positive signs of increased workplace activity were, however, tempered by the finding that in a number of cases, instead of the new types of continuous vocational training representing 'real' innovative training interventions, the 'new' training did not amount to anything more than a formalisation and standardisation of previously informal training processes.

'Learning organisations'

What is not known from these studies, or the national surveys, is what proportion of British companies has adopted policy and practices that bring them close to the model of learning organisations; that is to say, where continuous learning is an integral part of the workplace and, indeed, business strategy; where there is a premium placed on a stimulating environment with opportunities for learning; where an explicit process is in place for assessing training needs both for employers' succession planning and for the employee's career development planning; and where there is a strongly held commitment by senior management to the long-run competitive benefits of investing in people.

Research findings would appear to suggest that there are very few such firms, although many more might aspire to this ideal. An indicator of firms moving in this direction is the number involved in the Investors in People programme. So far, 2,725 employers, employing over 900,000 people, have met the standard and a further 17,500 organisations have made a public commitment to do so. Even so, these numbers fall well short of the National Education and Training Target for IIP of 70 per cent of organisations employing 200 people or more, and 35 per cent of those employing 50 or more, to be recognised by the year 2000. The current rate of achievement is 10 per cent and 6 per cent respectively. The evaluators of the IIP speculate that it may also be that views among the non-involved are polarising, with growing numbers unlikely to become involved (Hillage and Moralee, 1996).

Putting the ideas of the learning organisation into practice is an even more challenging task. Both the Tavistock and Raper studies observed a significant gap between the language or discourse of companies who viewed themselves as learning organisations and regarded people as their most important asset, and the actual practices of these companies. There is some evidence that suggests that sophisticated personnel management policies of the type espoused by Human Resource Management textbooks may be appropriate only to those product market strategies and production technologies and processes that demand workers with skills that are difficult to replace, and to workers who have jobs that could be redesigned to engender commitment and individual initiative (Lloyd and Rawlinson, 1992). There are sectors of the British economy where such conditions may not pertain.

Comparative studies

Most of the advanced industrial nations are seeing changes in the organisation of work, skill needs and new training and learning practices in both companies and vocational education training (VET) systems. Comparative data on workplace learning in Canada and the Netherlands – both countries with similar market-led training systems – provide a perspective on whether broad trends in the UK are running in parallel with those elsewhere.

No survey of the scale of on-the-job training is available for the Netherlands, although case studies and scattered evidence suggest that it occupies an important place in the overall provision of skills via company training. The main picture that emerges of the national system in the Netherlands is:

- a strong and steady rise in participation in company-offered training over the last 10 years, although not the same for all employee groups

- a clear tendency to strive for an integrated approach, involving both formal training and on-the-job learning

- the use of more structured on-the-job training for the acquisition of job-specific skills

- over-emphasis on structuring content and developing teaching materials for use in on-the-job training; insufficient attention to increasing the learning potential of jobs of the work process itself

- increased efforts to experiment with training of employees with low educational qualifications, and to integrate the training needs of rank-and-file production workers into global strategies of human resource management in the company

- increased emphasis of in-company training schemes on more practice-oriented, tailored training and at the same time a replacement of learning-by-doing in some vocational training courses by classroom-based teaching of theoretical concepts.

Onstenk (1997a) also observes that most of the learning and training opportunities in Dutch companies are determined by strictly economic and market-related considerations, ie what will enhance the nation's and/or company's competitiveness. While there are cases where the individual is encouraged to participate in learning more fully, these are the exception rather than the norm and apply to only a very small proportion of the company.

In Canada, a new source of information on workplace training is the Workplace Training Survey (WST), carried out in 1995 and 1996. Incorporating surveys and case studies, the WST collected data from employers and employees in every part of the country and virtually all industries. The main findings were that:

- some 70 per cent of companies undertook some training over the preceding 12-month period, but in many of these firms, this training was exclusively informal

- informal training accounts for the greater part of training, even in firms that conduct formal training as well

- highly skilled and educated employees are most likely to get training through their employer. This was true on an overall basis and for a wide range of specific types of programmes, including training for teamwork, problem-solving and communication, for management and supervisory skills, and for new technology

- training is strongly associated with innovation. Firms reporting significant technological change, 'high performance' human resource practices, and organisational changes to increase flexibility are firms that also report a lot of training

- the two other factors associated with high levels of training activity in firms are: competing in global markets and having a union

- trends over a two-year period indicate that firms may be increasingly segmented into two groups, one with a strengthening commitment to formal training, and the other with a weakening commitment. Firms that dropped formal training were more likely to be small, single-establishment firms, without unions

- not many firms can be characterised as 'learning organisations'; those that are tend to be large organisations.

Who benefits from learning at work?

Empirical evidence suggests there still exists a major learning divide in the workplace. Those who have fewer skills and are at the lower end of hierarchies or authority, autonomy and pay, also enjoy fewer formal opportunities for learning through work (Fryer, 1997). In a study undertaken for the Kennedy Report, NIACE found that more than half of all unskilled and semi-skilled workers said they had not participated in any learning at all since leaving full-time education, compared with under one-fifth of professionals and managers. Four-fifths of those who say they have not participated in learning since school think it is unlikely that they will do so in the future (Sargent et al, 1997).

The Labour Force Survey too shows that those in professional, associated professional and technical occupations are twice as likely as those in clerical, secretarial, personal, protective and craft jobs to have training provided by employers, and are more than four times as likely to do so as plant and machine operatives. Some employers who do not train employees at lower levels assume that they will not be interested, though it is clear from many studies that many of them are. Those who have no qualifications may be harder to get involved in training, but arguably they constitute the greatest area of wasted potential.

Job-related training may or may not lead to qualifications being awarded. The Labour Force Survey asks those who are doing job-related training whether it leads to a qualification, a credit for qualification, or neither. The results indicate a notable tendency towards having relatively more short courses of training, and although there is a continued expansion in training for qualifications, the fact that many of these qualifications are being achieved for very short courses of training suggests they are not of particularly high standard. Only a small proportion of those employees in training are working towards qualifications that would seem to equip them for the sorts of high skill/technological frontier jobs upon which it is regularly said that future prosperity depends (Felstead and Green, 1996).

These macro-level findings of a learning divide are found in other countries as well. In Canada, the Workforce Training Survey results confirmed other findings that the more highly skilled and educated employees are most likely to get training through their employer. Employees with a post-secondary education and in management or professional positions reported the highest training rates. This was true on an overall basis and for a wide range of specific types of programmes, including training for teamwork, problem-solving and communication, for management and supervisory skills, and for new technology.

Qualitative, descriptive research in the Netherlands shows that training for poorly educated employees, when they do receive training, consists mainly of company-specific, non-certificated short courses which do not have any market value outside the company, and as a consequence do not offer very much with respect to career possibilities. A large part of the training they receive is training on the job, sometimes under poor learning conditions.

Concluding comment

We do not yet have a clear picture of the extent to which the workplace is being used to support continuous vocational training and learning. In particular, we have a very incomplete picture of informal learning which is intrinsically linked to the day-to-day operations of the organisation. Most surveys gathering information on employers' training practices are premissed on a training paradigm, and while case study research provides a complementary picture it too tends to focus on the more structured kinds of workplace learning activity. There would seem to be relatively little understanding of the paradigmatic shift involved in looking at the workplace itself as a source of learning, whereby learning arises naturally out of the demands and challenges of work, and out of social interactions in the workplace with colleagues, customers and clients.

Research findings suggest that it is both unrealistic and unproductive to hold up the model of the learning organisation as an ideal. Its relevance is likely to be sector dependent as well as related to the size and complexity of the organisation. We need to understand better what kinds of organisations in which sectors have scope for increasing the learning potential of the workplace, and what the ingredients are in those organisations that have successfully transformed their workplaces into sites for learning. Case studies on a cross-sector basis are the most useful ones here.

In the chapters that follow, we look at what research has been undertaken that can tell us more about which organisations are most likely, and best placed, to introduce and support effective processes and structures for workplace learning. It is manifestly evident that there is great unevenness in the extent to which companies are making effective use of the workplace as a source for learning.

Chapter 3

Company strategies and sectoral differences

Chapter overview

- Unlike in Germany and Japan, the national learning culture in the UK does not engender a widespread commitment to learning in the workplace. Even so, it is clear that some UK companies train more than others, have a stronger commitment to the professional development of their workers, and make more effective use of the workplace as a source of learning. This leads us to ask what types of organisations are more likely to take workplace learning seriously, and why?

- Sectoral characteristics play a decisive role. Relevant factors include the industry culture, the competitive environment and product strategy, the use of new technology and labour market flexibility. Different industries face external pressures from their environment to varying degrees and are more or less open to intra-industry developments. It is evident that for some firms, heavy investment in workplace learning is not an appropriate (or the most appropriate) strategy for competitive positioning, although there may be other value-based reasons for creating a learning work environment.

- Size is clearly a strong determinant. Large organisations train more than small ones and more of their activity involves structured, planned training and learning. They are more likely to have sophisticated HRM strategies, to benchmark themselves internationally, and to be in a position to realise economies of scale from company-provided training. Regardless of size, however, those employers who have adopted some of the practices associated with the modern workplace are more likely to have formal training programmes.

- Multinational status, or association with international companies through franchising, supplier-chain relationships or other networking arrangements may differentiate a company from its industry competitors, driving niche marketing, branding and associated quality standards.

- Internal factors also play a role, notably the respective positions and discourses taken by key stakeholder groups. Trade-offs are involved in this interplay between competing management, worker and union interests. It is noticeable that those companies that have invested most heavily in employee development and training have done so simply as one part of a broader shift to very different models of industrial relations and personnel management which stress commitment, trust, good communications between management and employees, and the breakdown of status divides.

Industry culture, competitive environment and product strategy

Many of the external pressures on companies that we observed earlier in Chapter 2 are mediated by the industry sector. The sector gives particular shape to the predominant model of work organisation and the labour market strategy, both of which in turn influence the skill requirements of the workforce and the most effective way of meeting them. Traditions within the industry also play a role. Some industries are characterised by strong cultural attitudes and practices which ease or impede a transition to more modern forms of work organisation and which facilitate or inhibit learning in the workplace. However, these institutional factors are not deterministic. Some high-skill employers are driven by the competitive pressure of their particular market; others believe that this is the best way to attain competitive advantage. These institutional factors simply increase the probability that firms will invest in workforce development (Finegold and Levine, 1997).

Low-cost/low-skill strategies

The hospitality and catering industry well exemplifies a sector where the scope for workplace learning is limited, beyond responding to immediate pressures for customer care programmes (Tavistock Institute, 1998a). The whole sector is characterised by acute recruitment difficulties, high labour turnover, low pay, as well as poor working conditions and an increased use of casualised labour. Traditional ways of organising labour along the lines of a low-cost low-skill rationale have been broadly maintained. The model of work organisation is driven towards increasing the volume of sales and cost savings, reinforced by reliance on the external labour market for low skills labour. The sector has traditionally offered reduced opportunities for qualification and minimal career paths.

Case studies of companies in the sector demonstrate that while the quest for better service quality and customer service has led to structured 'customer care' training programmes, which are then further reinforced by management exhortations, this 'evangelical-style training' does not really filter through to workplace practice. This is principally because operational priorities and cost efficiency concerns take precedence.

The construction industry faces similar problems (Scott and Cockrill, 1997). The industry has one of the poorest images of all sectors, bedevilled by problems including inferior products, management and labour, and characterised generally by low technology, low trust and conflictual relationships. Taylorist work strategies have predominated, coupled with high labour turnover among poorly qualified staff and an emphasis on competition based on cost minimisation. The adversarial low trust relations between employers and employees has favoured the expansion of self-employment and the fragmentation of the craft trades.

There is little or no requirement for proof of skill to trade as a builder in the UK (unlike in Germany, where a Meister qualification is a prerequisite), and on the whole the take-up of NVQs has been used for either initial training or office staff training rather than in further development of construction work skills. Among a sample of 25 construction SMEs in South Wales, Scott and Cockrill found that the sector was overwhelmingly characterised by a voluntarist tradition of informal training, *ad hoc* in nature and transmitted entirely through 'learning by doing'. Despite pressures for multiskilling in some work environments (notably local authorities), little or no formal training of this kind is being provided. Firms in the construction industry take a predominantly reactive approach to further training and certification, propelled mainly by legislative and safety needs and, indeed, customer demands.

Official and semi-official bodies (Royal Academy of Engineering, 1996; Office of Science and Technology, 1995) have recently contended that the UK construction industry has so far failed to adopt, or even to study the potential of, techniques underlying the renaissance of competitiveness and performance of manufacturing. These include human resource development, greater use of new technology, customer focus, benchmarking, a total quality approach, continuous learning, and so on.

Companies in both the hospitality and construction industries would appear to have insufficient incentive to institute workplace learning practices beyond a minimal level. Their low-skills low-cost strategy is sufficient to maintain competitive position in a localised market. A combination of incidental learning on the job and event-triggered training in response to regulatory requirements meets most of the current training needs of workers who are generally unconcerned about qualifications.

Transformational strategy

A clustering of companies providing financial, banking and insurance services share sectoral characteristics that provide a more optimistic set of conditions for workplace learning (Eraut et al, 1998; Raper et al, 1997; Tavistock Institute,1998a). These industries are experiencing an ongoing and sometimes patchy shift from hierarchical organisational cultures built around administrative processes to more commercial, customer-oriented systems. Relationships with clients have become more important as expectations are higher and the competition is more intense. Companies resort both to internal and external labour market flexibility, although job shedding and delayering has meant significantly reduced recruitment as well as the disappearance of career paths.

Transformations have included:

- organisational transformation, such as the reorganisation of companies around front offices and the conversion of back offices into support centres with a customer-oriented ethos

- transformation of personnel management, including the disappearance of structured career paths according to seniority

- transformation of skill requirements, both deskilling and upskilling

- transformation of organisational culture from one of 'blame' associated with old rigid definition of roles to one encouraging individual initiative in line with the broader definition of responsibilities and teamwork.

The broad financial services industry is faced with oppositional tendencies. The introduction of information technology has meant that technical knowledge of the organisation increasingly resides in software systems, leading to a marked decrease in the level of discretion exercised by most workers. Banking used to be a career profession, involving moves through various banking operations towards posts carrying ever greater responsibility for the risks associated with lending to individuals and corporations. But it has now become a systems-led operation in which much of the discretion available to senior individuals has been removed by computer-based assessments capable of being undertaken by more junior staff.

On the other hand, the broadening of the financial services and products on offer, the importance of long-term relationships with customers, and the marketing judgements about the competitiveness of products, have created new training needs and skill requirements, particularly at the 'soft' end of selling and communication.

Training and workplace learning in this sector is both events driven as well as having some features of a more strategic approach. Training 'triggers' include the introduction of new products, quality procedures and systems (primarily focused on the individual and with emphasis on self-directed learning). Delayering, with supervisors assuming training responsibilities, has also prompted a training response. At the same time, training is also being driven by an emphasis on performance management systems involving target-setting and regular reviews of progress against a set of performance indicators. Some companies have mentoring schemes in place for graduate trainees.

Overall, the sector is characterised by a dual agenda of change and productivity/ profitability. Research studies suggest that the financial services area attaches importance to workplace learning, not only as a response to immediate pressures, but as part of the continuing updating and reskilling of the workforce. There is an element of continuous improvement of knowledge-based systems, with local knowledge of software systems being fed back to the systems designers, as well as an ongoing need for strong emphasis on quality of service as a key source of competitive advantage.

Continuous improvement strategy

The automotive industry is the archetypal exemplar of a 'TQM organisation' that has more fully internalised the rationale of the market and the supremacy of the customer than the other industry sectors/organisational types discussed above (Tavistock Institute, 1998a; Rosengarten, 1995; Danau and Sommerlad, 1996). The sector is characterised by intense competition, which focuses primarily on continuously improving product quality at increasingly lower costs. It is one of the sectors that particularly felt the full brunt of Japanese manufacturing in the 1970s and 1980s. This in turn led the sector to change its product configuration quite dramatically by the adoption of just-in-time production and delivery modes (Oliver and Wilkinson, 1988).

Companies in this sector include both the large manufacturers (Rover, Ford, Toyota, Nissan) as well as those supplying automotive components. Firms generally claim to have moved from Fordist techniques of mass production, characterised by semi-skilled work on an assembly line, to post-Fordist production, with multiskilled workers producing a more diversified range of products with shorter product life cycles. Among other things, this is achieved through the establishment of supply-chain relationships which blur the boundaries not only between organisations but also within the company. Suppliers and customers, both external and internal, become an integral part of the production process, thus resulting in a very close working relationship at all levels and on a wide range of issues, including training.

Case studies of six automotive components suppliers (Rosengarten, 1995) demonstrate the kinds of investments made in human capital that are indicative of a learning organisation. These include:

- the introduction of self-organising teamwork, as a replacement for a Tayloristic structure which included supervisors and foremen. Intra-organisational teams are predominantly continuous improvement teams and product development teams; inter-organisational teams are established for the co-operation with customers, suppliers and partner companies. These teams create free vertical and horizontal flow of information.

- a framework of support for continuous improvement teams, including the dissemination of new knowledge gained to other parts of the company

- job enlargement and job enrichment, achieved through multiskilling and job rotation

- decentralised hierarchies and participative management

- learning laboratories and constant experimentation, besides or as part of the normal production process

- learning reward systems for employees

- education and training of the whole workforce.

Workplace learning in this sector is inextricably linked to the achievement of business objectives, the result being a very integrated, regulated, formalised and standardised system of training which is expected to have a direct and immediate impact on production and work organisation. Company studies indicate large number of employees make use of the opportunity provided through company learning centres to work towards nationally recognised qualifications.

The clothing industry (Brown et al, 1994) shares some features with the automotive industry, although it is not as advanced along this path. The market environment has changed, with greatly increased emphasis upon more individualised and specialist products, and with quality overtaking cost as the decisive factor in the decision to purchase. Electronic data exchange means changes in the product can be accommodated rapidly and this in turn has led to a further segmentation of the retail market. Modular design and the use of a variety of standard components may allow a continuing degree of customisation around the basic design. The new production system is likely to involve modular manufacture or cellular production, with small working groups being involved in the production of whole garments, or alternatively some movement from cell to cell.

The emphasis upon quality, the ability to operate a number of machines and to work in a small team, to which a number of supervisory functions have been decentralised, all in turn require a new approach to learning and training systems. Greater skill and commitment are necessary. Alongside such internal pressures for a revision of staff development and training, external labour market conditions reinforce the centrality of developing and retaining a committed, highly skilled labour force.

Companies in industries facing global competition, the introduction of advanced technologies and strong internal and external customer demands are at the vanguard in introducing new forms of work organisation. The heavy investment in human capital, both in upskilling the workforce as well as developing an ethos of continuous improvement, imposes its own logic for fostering employee loyalty, commitment and job stability/security through learning organisation practices.

Sectoral comparisons

The importance of sectoral characteristics as a key determinant of the likely uptake of, and potential for, workplace learning has emerged in other country studies. The Workplace Training Survey conducted in Canada in every part of the country and in virtually all industries, showed the incidence of training to be highest in 'non-market' service industries (eg health and education). Training was also strongly associated with firms reporting significant technological change, 'high performance' human resource practices, and organisational changes to increase flexibility. High levels of training activity were also found in companies competing in global markets. The Tavistock Institute study of Continuing Vocational Training, undertaken in three countries across industry sectors, pointed to sectoral characteristics as being as important as, or even more important than, as the national and institutional frameworks within which companies operate.

A summary of the workplace learning arrangements found in different sector-based companies included within the research studies referred to above is provided in Figure 1 below.

Figure 1   Workplace learning innovations in sectoral studies of companies

	Case Study Sample	Strategy	CVT innovations/OJL
Automotive industry			
Tavistock Institute (1998a)	large auto components company	product innovation and quality, coupled with cost reduction	• learning centre • robotic simulators and related CBT training • TQM-related training • training role split from supervisory role

	Case Study Sample	Strategy	CVT innovations/OJL
Automotive industry (cont)			
Rosengarten (1995)	six auto components suppliers		• company-based provision of modular courses for E&T • in-house training combined with use of cassettes, interactive videos, laser discs • extension of training to suppliers in working/ problem-solving techniques • learning laboratories and experimentation • quality/safety-based training
Financial services/insurance/banking			
Eraut et al (1998)	three financial services organisations	strong customer service orientation	• workplace learning centre • open learning training packages • organised learning support: coaching, mentoring, induction
Tavistock Institute (1998a)	two leading insurance companies	product information and good customer service	• learning/staff development centre • CBT • learning contracts/ personal development plans • split of training role from managerial role
Raper et al (1997)	two leading banks		• training developed to line managers • job shadowing, mentoring • use of manuals, guides to support OJT • planned work experience • open learning, CBT
Construction			
Scott and Cockrill (1997)	25 construction SMEs	low skills/low cost	• training to meet regulatory requirements • reliance on outside bodies for training needs assessment and provision (CITG/CITB/FE) • limited use of NVQs • emphasis on 'learning by doing'

	Case Study Sample	Strategy	CVT innovations/OJL
Health care			
Eraut et al (1998)	three NHS Trusts based on district hopsitals	professional service/public sector efficiency	• just-in-time courses • coaching and mentoring • NVQs/formal study • team learing • learning from experts • self-directed learning
Retail			
Raper et al (1997)	two multiple branch high street stores		• informal learning on the job • coaching, for supervisor development • training of 'key operators' • open learning centre, CBT
Manufacturing			
Brown et al (1994)	three companies		• quality action teams • training of supervisor (master qualification) • supported OJT/OJL
Hospitality and catering			
Tavistock Institute (1998a)	two hotels, part of international hotel chain	service standardisation/ excellence	• career development centre • NVQs • split of training role from managerial role • learning contracts • training based on brand standards
Textiles			
Raper et al (1997)	two companies – one global with multiple sites, the other family run	low skill/low cost	• shift to self-directed learning • highly structured off-the-job training for new operatives • quality circles
Brown et al (1994)		quality/customer responsiveness/ high skill	• QA systems for suppliers • explicit development of team working skills • training to upgrade skill levels

Size differences

Surveys of training consistently show that large organisations train more than small ones, and more of their activity involves formal training. Despite the fact that small business is seen to offer the most effective outlets for fostering individual employee and employer growth (Hakim, 1989), training and human resource needs have not been prominent in the competitive agenda of small and medium enterprises.

Although there have been recent detailed studies of training patterns and training decisions of SME owner/managers in the UK (for example, Hyland and Matlay, 1997) these tend not to distinguish between external VET and company provided training. On-the-job learning has not been part of the conceptual framework. We thus have inadequate information on the SME sector about the relativities of off-the-job to on-the-job training or the forms that workplace learning takes. On the surface, the economic pressures that are driving large enterprises to favour decentralised on-the-job training that is incorporated into supervisory or team management roles would appear to be attractive also to SMEs, where work is organised in this way and where they take training seriously. Other training practices, such as job rotation or where workers need to be taken out of productive work for training, are less likely to be accommodated in firms of smaller size.

Recent research suggests that the SME managers learn and develop competences that relate to SME performance, not so much through formal training as through informal learning processes based on personal relationships and formal and informal networks (Hines and Thorpe, 1995; Cullen and Sommerlad, 1997; Cullen, 1998). This includes learning with and from customers, suppliers, owners, employees, environments and competition (Pedler et al, 1991). Informal learning, relating to the transfer of technical know-how, knowledge about markets and customer requirements, and other forms of business-related knowledge are seen as more timely and relevant to the needs and circumstances of SMEs than are training solutions.

In Japan, the level of sophistication of management methods and of skill development systems adopted by industry are in direct relationship to company size. Co-operative arrangements between SMEs are commonplace, however, with businesses grouping together in order to maximise resources and to gain the benefits of government training support. The incidence of companies offering off-the-job training is much less in SMEs than in large organisations. Planned job rotation and transfers provide an extended form of on-the-job training throughout working life in large companies, although the scope for this in small companies is more limited. Large companies frequently offer training places to smaller companies that are associated with them. (Oram, 1995)

The discourse of conflict and consensus

There is another dimension to the way in which different enterprises approach workplace learning, with learning being seen as predominantly a company or an individual responsibility. Workplace learning is a contested arena, in which the different agendas or discourses of the various actors are played out (Tavistock Institute, 1998a). In some companies, such as the TQM-led organisations, there is a dominant ideology of survival through competitiveness which is more or less shared by all participants, ie senior managers, line/departmental managers, training departments, trade unions and individual employees. The commitment to TQM and related CVT is articulated by the managing director, who in this way ensures there is 'one voice' to be heard within the company as far as staff training and development is concerned. Research suggests that the parties are willing to find trade-offs – a commitment to organisational and business goals (including continuing learning work) being offset against employment security, better salaries and intensive staff training and development.

In other companies, there is a multiplicity of contradictory 'voices' and agendas at play. Often, this was evident in tension between the human resource and/or training department (in most cases the driving force of CVT) on the one hand, and senior managers on the other. Among other things, this meant that despite the fact that management (often top and senior management) talked about and praised the importance of staff training and development, the organisational reality was that this remained at the level of rhetoric.

Many employers were using the discourse of 'employability' (legitimised by government policy) as a weak approach to human resource development. These employers make an implicit commitment to enhance the employability of their staff by providing mainly work-related CVT and by setting up a 'training infrastructure' (exemplified by the proliferation of manned and unmanned learning centres). In exchange, employees accept the lack of any guarantee for lifetime employment and try to remain 'employable' by making maximum use of existing training opportunities and facilities. In such a context, 'employability' is seen as being ultimately a responsibility of the individual and not of the company.

Chapter 4

Approaches to learning at work

Chapter overview

- Learning at work encompasses many different learning processes. These are difficult to categorise and compare as they are grounded in different paradigms of learning, have different goals, are associated with different kinds of activities, and are centred on different levels of the organisation – from the individual, to the team and through to the organisation. Learning may be primarily oriented towards employee development, or it may be more narrowly concerned with employers' business goals. The outcomes of learning may manifest as knowledge or skill development by the individual or as knowledge that is incorporated into organisational memory, routines and procedures through a cycle of continuous improvement and knowledge creation. Some learning processes, moreover, are clearly bounded and separated out from other activities with an explicit pedagogic intent and structure, while others are integrated into work organisation and production processes.

- A further difficulty in reviewing the research literature is that empirical studies have very different starting points, and thus approach learning processes from different angles. There is, for instance, a substantial body of research concerned with the development of core competences in the workplace. The focus is generally on the individual, with core competences typically understood as the set of personal skills, attributes and dispositions that underpin the capacity to act in a responsible manner with regard to complex work tasks. One line of research enquiry pursued by those researchers interested in core competences or core skills has been to explore which kinds of competences are best developed in which learning settings, and what kinds of learning processes are involved.

- Another starting point is the set of training and education initiatives that are packaged as 'employee development' schemes in the workplace and which are primarily centred on the personal development of employees. ED schemes may encompass job-related learning but are broader than job-specific training. They seek to encourage a positive attitude towards learning, particularly among those who have traditionally been excluded from vocational education and training. Studies of these initiatives tend to focus on the aims, organisational frameworks and outcomes, with only secondary interest in the processes involved in adults learning in the workplace. The workplace is viewed more as a site for learning than as a source of learning.

- A new wave of empirical research has addressed the relationship between technological–organisational redesign, changes in work organisation and employee competence development. Studies of this kind are concerned with learning processes, which are embedded in the design of the workplace and the production of work itself. Common configurations include cellular manufacturing techniques, teamwork and group work, quality improvement teams and multi-skilling and job rotation.

- Finally, our view of how learning in the workplace is planned and structured is complemented by research which starts at the other end, as it were. Recently undertaken research, taking a learner-centred approach, has focused on the learning experiences and aspirations of employees themselves and the ways in which they were able to take advantage of learning opportunities in the workplace.

- Taken together, the findings from these overlapping domains of research help to build up a picture of the very diverse kinds of strategies or processes that have been used to structure learning in the workplace or which might be further exploited in the future.

The workplace as a site for the development of core competences

The interest in core competences arises from recognition that the occupational demands of the modern workplace can no longer be met through specialised occupational knowledge and skills alone. Workers within a post-Fordist industrial structure require a set of core skills or competences which do not become outdated and which underpin flexibility, adaptability and transferability.

Researchers have conceptualised 'core competences' in a variety of different ways (Danau and Sommerlad, 1996). The Confederation of British Industry, in its report on Flexible Labour Markets (1994) takes a 'core skills' approach which identifies such skills as literacy, numeracy, personal and social skills, problem-solving skills and IT literacy. In many countries it is assumed that these basic skills will be developed in the school system and are thus not the concern of the workplace. Their relevance for vocational training in the UK reflects the high proportion of early school leavers in the workforce, many of whom have serious deficiencies in core skills of literacy and numeracy – reflecting earlier failures in the full-time education system. In the British view, core competences tend to be seen in terms of a threshold standard rather than as subject to continuous improvement.

In Japan, in contrast to the UK, the large majority of those entering the workforce bring to the workplace a high level of abstract and symbolic thinking, as well as social skills and behaviours that are well attuned to the team-working environment. Japanese models of skill formation and competency development place strong emphasis on intellectual skill, which Koike and Inoke (1990) define as the 'knowledge to handle changes and problems associated with new integrated systems of production'. This calls for knowledge of:

- the process – its layout, sequence of events and interdependencies

- the product – its key characteristics and properties

- the equipment – its functions, capabilities and limitations, and

- the controls – the effect of control actions on performance.

At a holistic level, workers need to understand the logic of the production process, seeing it not as a discrete set of activities but as a network of complex operations.

The process by which intellectual skills are developed in Japanese workers is continuous, and entails both formal and informal modes of learning.

An innovative approach to the development of intellectual/cognitive skills among employees in an automated/computer-controlled workplace is described by Schuck (1996), drawing on research in four North American industrial organisations in which computer-based technology was being used to automate the manufacturing process. Her study, described in the box below, focuses on the process of learning intellectual skill and ways in which that learning can be enhanced.

A new pedagogy for the development of intellectual skill

Typically, training for new technology focuses on precise and well-defined applications. Training is task specific, highly structured, and occurs in a classroom setting. Workers are given information on a 'need to know' basis. They learn just enough about the equipment, the process and the terminal operations to be able to monitor and control their area of responsibility. Training is generally reactive. When the process or the equipment changes, new objects and actions are taught.

This traditional pedagogy offers little or no opportunity for learning the intellectual skill needed to make new meaning out of the data generated by the technology. Managers in some plants have recognised the need for ongoing training to increase the knowledge of workers and have designed 'job rotation' or 'cross-skilling' programmes in which the worker learns to operate another piece of equipment or to function in a different area in the process. These programmes expand the worker's repertoire of objects and actions, but they are of limited value in the IT-intensive workplace if they do not provide opportunities to learn and use intellectual skill. Intellectual skill involves learning how to think, developing a capability for independent problem-solving and moving from the level of objects and actions to the level of meaning.

Training for highly automated workplaces requires a pedagogy that creates an environment conducive to the development of intellectual skill. There is a reconceptualisation of the workplace as a learning environment and a redefinition of the role of manager in the learning process. The first step is to create an environment that supports inquiry. True inquiry is dependent on the motivation and curiosity of the learner, and the best time to learn is at the exact moment when you are faced with a real problem or question. A pedagogy for meaning focuses on the learner's question and is most concerned with ongoing learning in the natural environment. Companies are adopting a variety of strategies that acknowledge that learning is socially mediated: assigning 'partners' to work together at terminals; making available a budget for travel to other companies, vendors, or customer organisations; equipping a library that makes information and expert knowledge available to workers through a wide variety of media and using computer technology itself as a vehicle for ongoing dialogue as well as for computer simulations.

Whether people respond to a workplace designed to support inquiry depends largely on the quality of social interactions and attitudes of workers and managers. The manager of inquiry encourages people to ask questions and

---

creates an environment in which intellectual play and socially mediated learning are necessary and legitimate components of work. Managers and workers become partners in an ongoing learning process. Designing formal reward systems that stimulate, encourage and recognise inquiry and learning is also essential in such work places.

The approach to learning is very different from what we have come to expect from terms like 'teaching' and 'training'. These words usually connote situations in which there are clearly defined roles. In the new pedagogy, learning is a collective activity in which the focus is on asking questions and engaging in dialogue, and roles are not predetermined but are fluid and dependent on individuals' expertise and insight in a particular situation.

Only through the application of intellectual skill can people perceive the meaning of the data in an automated and information-rich environment and make conscious and intelligent choices to solve problems or to identify more efficient or effective approaches to the business.

Source: Schuck (1996)

Recent European approaches to core competences reflect a shift away from defining competences as a bundle of discrete skills to a more holistic contextualised approach. A number of different categorisations have been put forward (Bunk, 1994; EUROTECNET, 1993; Onstenk, 1993) which emphasise the interdependence between social, methodological, technical and participatory modes of competence. These are seen to underpin the capacity to act in a responsible manner in a complex work environment. Employees are expected to be able to troubleshoot and solve problems; to be prepared for self-directed learning; to be active contributors to dialogue between team members; and to respond quickly to changing work requirements. Onstenk (1992) emphasises in addition the importance of 'transfer skills' or a kind of metacompetence which supports the transferability of knowledge and know-how from the situation in which they were acquired to new work roles and tasks. Such skills need to be developed and applied continuously as an individual employee moves from novice to expert.

Vocational research has been concerned with how these competences can best be developed through varying combinations of off-the-job training in a vocational centre, near-the-job training in a simulated work environment, on-the-job training and real productive work. Different countries give different weight to these elements, depending on the level of skill developed in the school system, the nature of the vocational training system, the relative importance attached to some aspects of core competence development over others and the distribution of responsibilities between the state and the employer for skill formation. In Japan, the acquisition of these skills and competences is embedded in a process of company socialisation. In Sweden, strong emphasis is put on the communicative and participatory modes of competence linked to democratisation and democratic dialogue in the firm. In the Netherlands, change is underway in pushing back some areas of competence development from the workplace to the classroom, where it is considered they can best be acquired.

In Germany, there has been concern that current arrangements for vocational training under the dual system have given insufficient attention to social learning models, which are seen as increasingly important in the modern workplace. The current view is that learning to live and work as a team cannot be taught, it can only be learned by being part of a team. The concept of 'learning islands' was introduced as one of a number of 'prototype' forms of work organisation to test their practical feasibility as a tool for developing occupational competence for work roles of the future (Dehnbostel, 1996). [1] See box below.

The learning island, set up in a company setting, is integrated into the production process, spatially and organisationally. Wherever possible, this organisational integration is part of the real production process with the same conditions, problems and working procedures. Activities that are to be carried out are focused on real production that requires quality and economic value, so no laboratory or simulation exercises are involved. The pedagogic goal of learning islands is to develop the skills of workers in a broad sense: task-oriented competencies, planning skills, responsibility and social skills. Work in the learning island is project-oriented and the group decides autonomously how they wish to realise the project.

Learning islands – a German innovation in workplace vocational training

In the Mercedes-Benz plant, learning islands have been set up with three different objectives in mind:

- to develop the technical and social skills of employees

- to accustom employees to team working

- to learn from alternative organisational forms and structures to shape the organisation in the future.

The learning islands are located in a separate section of the work floor which contains production and educational facilities. To exploit the strengths of semi-autonomous work groups fully, learning islands are created in the places of the production where complex tasks need to be carried out. In these islands, employees work in teams on integrated and complex tasks (project-oriented). These tasks include planning and solving logistical problems. The semi-autonomous working groups are supported by a mentor who co-ordinates and intervenes only when it is really necessary.

Prior to the start, the group is given clearly defined goals that need to be realised in the working period of five weeks. To encourage employees to look for improvements, feedback about the progress made is given regularly to the group.

---

[1] A characteristic feature of the German vocational education system is the high level of interest in prototype projects and experiments. A major part of the government programme is concerned with experiments which are then widely publicised by means of extensive evaluation, reports and guidelines.

Learning islands are not only located in companies characterised by post-Fordist modes of production. One of the reasons for having these experimental learning islands close to employees who are not yet involved in a team-based working is that it is hoped that in this way these employees will identify themselves with the initiatives and become familiar with the process of change. In this way, it is hoped that resistance to change will be reduced.

In the Daimler-Benz training centre in Gaggenau, the mentors are selected by senior workers and are rostered off the production line to support employees in the learning islands. The 'learning island' team group is responsible for compensating for the loss of productive labour of their mentor within this period. In this way, it is made clear to the young workers what it means to work in an industrial commercial context. The mentor's role is that of counsellor: s/he functions as contact point for the group but intervenes only when serious errors are made. The intention here is to preserve the autonomy of the group as far as possible.

Another methodology aimed at developing the core competences and skills that are needed for flexible manufacturing is known as Leittext. Originally developed at the Daimler-Benz training centre, it is used in a variety of companies in Germany as well as in the Netherlands, where it has been taken up by Philips. It is seen as having particular relevance for low-skilled workers and trainees, where the intention is to develop workers' capability to plan, execute and monitor their work independently The Leittext method is described in the box below.

The Leittext method

The Leittext method is a structured form of job training carried out near to the job, which begins with trainer-guided phases of theoretical and practical instruction that progressively phase into trainee-managed activities. A Leittext is built around a task that can be unfolded in partial steps. Material that is already part of the workplace is used as far as possible. It consists of an introductory text which gives the trainee a precise explanation of the purpose of the material being tackled and the Leittext questions. These questions are based on analyses of the activity that is to be carried out, the know-how that is needed to carry out the task and the corresponding information that is needed to acquire the knowledge. The role of the trainer is focused on activities that stimulate the trainee by developing 'Leittext questions', discussions of intermediate results of the trainee's activities, and providing support during the learning process. In practice, the role of the trainer is shared by trainers and workers.

Developing a learning workforce through employee development schemes

Employee development learning programmes (EDs) emerged in Britain towards the end of the 1980s and were much influenced by the North American examples from the early 1980s. Programmes in the auto industry in particular are well known, notably UAW-FORD in collaboration with the University of Michigan in the US, and the Ford Motor Company's joint Employee Development and Assistance Programme (EDAP) in the UK. The early programmes were the forerunners of the (open) learning centres which are today associated with many UK companies.

These are primarily educational schemes which emphasise the personal development of employees. They may encompass job-related learning but are always broader than job-specific training. They provide learning opportunities for substantial groups within the labour force previously excluded from education and often from job-specific training as well, especially those with limited previous education. Employee development schemes emphasise choice on the part of learners and provide continuous learning opportunities rather than one-off training events. They involve employees and/or their trade unions in the development of schemes and establish the rights of individuals to benefit from education organised in or through the workplace.

The motives surrounding the origins and subsequent development of these schemes remain complex. There has been a strong industrial relations impetus for ED, although in Britain the 'joint' element involving both employers and trade unions is far weaker than in the United States (Feerman et al, 1991). Instead, there is in the UK a dominant 'human resource' development perspective, seen as an important element in a longer-term strategic corporate vision (Forrester et al, 1993). Many of the firms introducing ED early on did so as a response to problems of high turnover, absenteeism, low morale and a host of other management problems. The programme was also shaped by the weakness of the compulsory and post-compulsory education systems in the UK, the lack of positive attitudes towards training on the part of employers, and the importance for employees to invest in their own learning. The missing millions of employees, or the 70 per cent who received no recent training or education opportunities at work or elsewhere in Britain, was a driving force behind this new approach to vocational education and training. This accounts for the strong emphasis on the development of basic (remedial) skills along with the concern to instil more positive attitudes towards continuing learning as part of developing a 'learning culture' in the workplace.

ED programmes work alongside company-based training programmes rather than substituting for them. Typically, they include a variety of education and training opportunities that are offered off-site in the workplace learning centre, generally in the employee's own time. Learning programmes include basic skills training (numeracy, literacy, communication, IT skills), language courses, self-development and skills enrichment courses, home improvement and vocational training.

Forrester et al, (1993, 1995a, b) undertook a two-year research project into the nature and growth of ED learning programmes in the workplace. Their findings are based on a survey of 70 firms which had set up such schemes or were regarded as leaders in the field of training, supplemented by case studies in 11 companies. Their study revealed two main approaches to employee development, which they label the 'super-trainers' and the 'personal developers'.

Firms taking the first approach emphasise teamwork, IT applications, multi-tasking and multi-skilling. They normally have an open learning centre, and provide advice and guidance to employees. This may, in turn, be related to the annual appraisal system. They do not usually have trade union involvement in training. They do not normally emphasise personal development as an objective or, if they do, place it in a narrow HRM context which is more concerned with the firm's needs than employees' needs.

The firms characterised as 'personal developers' are remarkably similar to the 'super-trainers' in terms of working methods and training approach. However, in contrast, they are much more likely to have trade union involvement and are normally able to separate out the budget for ED from the general training budget. Their approach emphasises the personal development of employees, offers choice of subjects to be studied and establishes an element of entitlement to education. ED may include job-specific training but its scope broadens to include opportunities for broader personal development through education.

The case study described in the box below is an exemplar of the personal developer approach to employee development.

Case study of employee development in Baxi Heating

Baxi Heating, employing 1,050 workers, is the market leader in domestic central heating products. Founded in 1866, the company changed its status in 1983 and is now owned by the employees. The business was reorganised in 1990 with the introduction of strategic business units, the replacement of a whole layer of supervisory management by team working and team leaders, and the implementation of a continuous improvement programme.

Baxi is committed to the development of its employees as an essential strategy for remaining competitive. As staff turnover is practically nil, the company cannot rely on new entrants as a source of new skills but must therefore train and retrain its own staff on a continuing basis. The long-term objective is to have an educated and adaptable workforce and to create a learning environment in which workers are encouraged to take up training opportunities, both vocational and non-vocational.

An open learning centre was set up, offering a range of basic skills, language and other courses identified through a training needs analysis. These include team leader training, appraisal, absence control, counselling and a wide range of job-specific F/HE courses. Courses are open to all employees with their team leader's agreement, are free and take place 50:50 in company and the individual's own time.

Shortly after the courses started, the company underwent a major reorganisation which reduced the workforce by 100 people. Employees were fearful of admitting to basic skills problems, and also a fear of being seen 'off the job'.

The development of workplace education is perceived by the company as an essential part of its 'partnership culture'. In the several years it has now been operating, the company believes it has increased workers' motivation, raised levels of self-esteem, improved communication skills and empowered team members. Employees have increased confidence to respond to the new demands of team working, continuous improvement and active involvement in workplace decision-making, after years of being treated as 'hands', not brain.

The company has also seen a significant improvement in the industrial relations climate, with not one failure to agree registered for over two years. It attributes this to the joint trade union/management approach. Other benefits include improved team building and understanding of the business, an increased take-up of job-related training, and employees taking the initiative in developing their own potential and career. A benefit for the company has been the recruitment advantages, with the initiative enhancing the company's image and directly attracting applicants, who see a progressive company dedicated to training.

The company is investing very heavily in training over the next five years, each provision being identified in the strategic medium-term plan. 'We have learnt from the open learning basic education programme that opportunities which go beyond the immediate needs of the job can inspire greater employee interest in learning and promoting adaptability.'

Forrester et al, (1995b) were surprised by the frequency with which the expected benefits identified by employees matched those described by managers. The 'mutual benefits' of ED schemes were seen as improved performance at work, greater satisfaction and motivation, and an opportunity to further develop a career, either within or outside the firm. Similar benefits were seen to accrue to the firm: the worker was seen as more committed and more open to change. It is this mutual benefit which makes employee development schemes an attractive option for companies wanting to move away from management–labour conflict. However, no company visited as part of the study by Forrester and colleagues was able to provide any evidence substantiating the claims for the improvements flowing from ED. In fact, no company visited had any monitoring or evaluation systems in place.

Innovation, work teams and learning on the job

The new organisational paradigm emphasises the connections between innovation, company policies and training and learning. Changes in technology, organisational renewal, optimisation of the quality of production and orientation to changing customer demands call for continuous learning on the part of the workers at the same time as creating new opportunities for learning. In theory, then, there is potential for realisation both of increased efficiency of production as well as of a more humane, people-oriented work organisation which enhances employee empowerment and professional development. However, it would appear that most companies have no real idea of the organisational changes that are necessary to create an environment of continuous learning work, partly because this often represents a complete break with tradition and there are few ready-made strategies and examples to hand (Onstenk, 1997b).

A distinction is commonly made between on-the-job training and on-the-job learning, with the latter being equated with continuous learning work. In reality, innovations in workplace learning that are associated with new forms of work organisation and production processes tend to merge these two. On-the-job training and on-the-job learning can both be planned and structured by an underlying pedagogy, although it may be more evident in some kinds of on-the-job training. Recent interest in how the learning potential of the small work group can be extended and developed is an example of the merging of training and learning concepts.

Working in teams as a learning strategy

Common new modes of work organisation include teamwork and group work, cellular manufacturing techniques, product/customer groupings and quality circles and improvement teams. Introducing the small work group as a leading organisational principle has several objectives. The first and most important one is to increase organisational productivity. The work group introduces flexibility through multi-skilling, creates links across functions and organisational boundaries, allows team members to deal on the spot with production problems that have become harder to predict because of small batch sizes and fast renewal of technology and products, and gives employees a broader view of the production process and of where they fit into the system (Neumann, Holti and Standing, 1995).

A second objective for introducing small work groups concerns the management of human resources. Team working is seen as enhancing motivation, improving the quality of labour and lowering absenteeism. Job enlargement and enrichment are not so much aimed at improving the work process as stimulating motivation, responsibility and self-esteem of employees. Working in small groups is also believed to strengthen group cultures in the company, facilitating socialisation and developing social–communicative skills. Lawler (1986) comments that 'Overall, work teams make an important difference in the participative structure of organisations. Individuals end up with knowledge and skills, information, rewards and power that they do not have in traditional organisations. Thus, work teams are likely to have an important positive impact on organisational effectiveness.'

A third objective, which has recently received more attention, entails using the small group as an explicit learning strategy. This can be at two levels, individual and collective. The small work group as a strategy for the development of individual competence places emphasis on such aspects as job rotation, task enrichment, problem-solving and mutual learning processes. The collective level is concerned with continuous improvement, whereby the tacit and often highly subjective insights, intuitions and hunches of individual employees are made available for testing and use by the company as a whole. Teams are seen as an effective way to stimulate organisational innovation, since they bring together complementary skills and experiences out of which new products can be created (Andrews, 1979).

Onstenk (1997b) is interested in how the work team can be designed and managed so as to optimise the potential for learning. Drawing together his findings from research in Dutch firms, he identifies the following as being important:

- broadening the set of tasks undertaken by the team so that there is scope for performing more tasks, eg by rotation to the work posts within the group

- enriching the job through integrating simple maintenance, repair and quality control tasks into the job

- giving the group responsibility for problem-solving as well as extending the domain of authority to make decisions

- organising team meetings and discussion opportunities which allow team/cross-team members to learn from one another and to come up with ideas for improvement

- structuring the composition of groups to include employees with different qualifications (content and level) in the work group

- including coaching of colleagues and team members as an explicit part of job descriptions.

The first case study example below illustrates the way in which the new integrated factory of Fiat has attempted to integrate these learning principles into the new production process and work organisation. Innovations of this kind are not, however, confined to the auto industry. Onstenk (pers comm) describes a number of companies in the Netherlands that are successfully introducing these concepts, including a textile printing company, an industrial bakery and a paper coating and printing factory. The second example, included as a case study (Tavistock Institute, 1998b) concerns the experience of a Dutch factory for cementing and jointing products.

Learning through team working: the Fiat example

The Fiat Melfi plan is the first example of the new production concept adopted by Fiat in the 1990s – the integrated factory. The new philosophy of integration seeks to reconcile a high-tech infrastructure with elements of the job shop (chiefly working in teams).

The factory is divided into four operating units (OUs) responsible for the different stages of the production process: pressing, body welding, painting and assembly. The four OUs co-operate in defining the daily production plan, monitoring the advancement of production, and managing the critical situations/problems. Each OU is divided into a number of working teams comprising between 20 and 40 workers and supervisors, responsible for one or more production lines. Specific objectives and results are assigned to each team and it is expected to solve (or contribute to solving) all problems that may hinder production, and to maintain quality control.

There are two principal strategies for learning: coaching and job rotation, and guided growth.

Coaching

Coaching is a team matter and is undertaken through mentoring, imitation and job rotation. Depending on their role and level of competence, newcomers may be assigned a permanent or temporary companion to guide their learning. Continuous rotation of generic workers over different posts ensures each member is capable of occupying each work post. Each work post is also identified by one or more panels hanging above the post which depicts

---

graphically the different steps required to perform an operation, which tools must be used and how, and what pieces/components are to be assembled. These panels are updated as a consequence of:

- the identification of a more appropriate way of carrying out the operation

- the identification of a default caused by the previous way of performing the operation.

As a worker masters a new skill, the accomplishment is listed next to his or her name on a skill development chart posted on a notice board.

Guided growth of a team

A second feature of 'learning embedded in the production process' is the guided learning process which is facilitated by two tutors who work with a team over an average period of 12 to 15 days. The main goals are:

- to help the team develop learning processes and methodologies

- to help it to develop a systemic understanding of the production processes

- to help it to solve everyday problems such as breakdowns on the production line

- to increase the efficiency of the whole system, not to teach a specific kind of task or job.

Once the tutor has finished working with the team, the team leader assumes responsibility for the management of the group and continues the activity of the tutor.

As a support for problem-solving, a manual which includes 28 methodologies of problem-solving, descriptions, software tools, etc has been developed for tutors' use in their role as agents of continuous change and catalysts for the learning process.

Source: Danau and Sommerlad (1996)

The factory for cementing and jointing products

In a factory producing cementing and jointing products which works directly for the consumer market, a radical change in job structure and quality improvement has been carried out, without a far-reaching innovation in the production process itself having taken place. Although parts of the process have been automated, there are still various approaches to process and production control, many of which are manually controlled. Innovation relates chiefly to the monitoring and improvement of quality.

The task group concept has been introduced in the first phase of the process of change. This implied adding minor maintenance and quality control functions to the production process. Daily production planning is also carried out on the shop floor in the new structure. This work organisation leads to more varied work, more complex and more broadly composed tasks, and more autonomy and scope. There is consequently a greater need for an understanding of the process and of quality and safety aspects. The emphasis is on on-the-job training under the guidance of an experienced colleague, combined with job rotation. The staff assessment system explicitly includes both attending training and work-based learning (particularly through task and job rotation) and contributing to learning processes of others. In this way, the acquired knowledge is also evaluated, recorded and rewarded particularly through the job structure and the assessment system.

Source: Tavistock Institute, 1998b

Continuous learning on the job offers learning opportunities to employees. At the same time, however, it is not without problems and risks. The small work group can enhance considerably the learning opportunities on the shop floor, but in many cases qualification processes are not central. Because the qualification function is not the first objective of the small work group, a tension with formal qualification trajectories can be expected. Training by rotation or mutual support can be threatened by work pressure or personnel shortages. In many cases, not enough attention is paid to the role of managers as 'facilitators' of learning processes. The same is true for the development of the 'colleague as trainer'.

It can also be a mistake to move too rapidly to a new mode of work organisation, as the following case study example illustrates. More importantly still, it highlights the importance of involving employees in innovation processes and redesign of work.

Introducing self-managing teams at a manageable pace

In a Dutch textile printing company, a radical (but unsuccessful) attempt to introduce self-managing teams led a sister company in the same holding company to choose less ambitious work reorganisation. Instead, it concentrated on designing a structure and learning process that fostered more gradual team autonomy and self-management, allowing for differences in speed and depth of change between teams in response to differences in skill level and production processes. This proved to be a successful strategy. Some teams are already de facto self-managing teams, reporting to the production manager and not to an appointed team leader or supervisor; others are still managed by a team leader or supervisor but are taking on team responsibility for specific tasks such as maintenance planning or quality improvement. All teams show a tendency to multi-skilling and increased learning at team level.

Source: cited in Onstenk, 1997a

Employees have to learn to participate in group processes and to recognise learning opportunities. Both are a necessary precondition for learning to take place, and also to do the job. In order to be effective in their roles, teams and team members not only need technical, functional or job competences but also team, interactive, interpersonal, communication competences, and action, problem-solving and decision-making skills (Katzenbach and Smith, 1993). There is very little empirical research on how these competences are best acquired and developed on a continuing basis.

OJL is structured by the organisation of labour as well as by guidance and support of the learning process by managers, trainers and colleagues. Learning and learning opportunities depend not only on the design of the job, but are also closely connected to changes in style of leadership and responsibilities, to the trajectory of change and more generally to skill formation processes in the company. The consequences of this for the integration of a Human Resources Management policy in the company policy as a whole are insufficiently recognised. Management still often lacks imagination for the integration of learning and working.

Creating opportunities for exchange and mutual learning

Action learning and study circles are techniques or methods that are used in the workplace as a major vehicle for development and change (McGill and Beaty, 1992; Weinstein, 1995). Although action learning is usually supported by colleagues, the process is focused on the individual. It involves a group of people – called a set – working together for a certain period of time on the work-based issues brought by each individual. The group is thus used as a resource or instrument for individual decision-making.

Action learning is best understood as initiating a process of doing things differently and/or behaving differently (Weinstein, 1995). Proponents of action learning claim that when action learning becomes a feature of the organisation itself, and many people take part in the action learning groups, the organisation itself, takes on some of the features of a learning organisation.

Study circles share common features with action learning. Swedish working life has considerable experience of the use of study circles to develop knowledge and skills among workers. As part of the Swedish Learning at Work Programme, a diverse group of companies, including hospitals, social security offices, Volvo and SECO Tools, experimented with the use of 'circles' to foster mutual learning as a basis for organisational learning.

The circles are composed of representatives of management and unions, and/or representatives of different functions in the organisation. The issue focused in the circle may be one in which the company has a lack of necessary knowledge and experience on which to base its decisions. External researchers and consultants may be invited to provide state-of-the-art knowledge and experience. The character of the circle is intended to develop from an active seeking through learning, problem formulation, problem-solving and finally implementation.

Other examples of such circles are 'experience circles' and corporate arenas in which experiences gained in different parts of the company are exchanged and evaluated for the benefit of the company as a whole. A further example is quality circles, for example in connection with companies' involvement in the ISO 9000 programme, which have been taken up in several countries with differing degrees of success.

A learner-centred perspective on what is learned at work

The recent study by Eraut and his team (1998), involving interviews with 120 managers, professionals and technicians in the engineering, business and healthcare sectors, started from a learning rather than a training perspective on workplace learning. The findings from this study offer insights into the kinds of workplace learning that is outside much human resource development thinking and planning. There are implications here for companies wishing to optimise the workplace as a site for learning.

Adopting a learner-centred perspective showed that formal education and training provide only a small part of what is learned at work. Most of the learning described by their interviewees was non-formal, neither clearly specified nor planned. It arose naturally out of the demands and challenges of work – solving problems, improving quality and/or productivity, or coping with change – and out of social interactions in the workplace. The outcome of such 'learning from experience' was the development of knowledge, skills and understanding, although this was difficult to explain to others. Effective learning was, however, dependent on confidence, motivation and capability – prerequisites for employees' self-management of much of their learning.

Formal training played a part – whether short courses, working for qualifications, distance learning or the use of written and audio-visual materials. Other structured learning supports, such as mentoring, shadowing, coaching and apprenticeship and trainee schemes, were also significant, especially where they were arranged locally.

Overall, their findings suggest an interplay between the formal and the informal, the importance of employee dispositions and core competences as a bedrock for learning, the matching of different combinations of formal and informal learning opportunities to career stages and changing job role responsibilities and the critical role of the local manager in establishing a climate favourable to learning.

Employees were purposeful about their learning, identifying learning goals which they pursued by a combination of self-directed learning and taking advantage of relevant learning opportunities as and when they appeared. This sometimes involved undertaking some formal training, but almost always required learning from experience and learning from other people at work. Learning from other people was sometimes facilitated by organised learning support, which could be formally organised by the Centre or organised informally at local level.

The former included apprenticeships and trainee schemes; while mentoring, shadowing and coaching were more likely to be locally arranged. The most common form of learning from other people took the form of consultation and collaboration within the immediate working group. This may include teamwork, ongoing mutual consultation and support or observation of others in action. Then, beyond the immediate work environment, people sought information and advice, often on a reciprocal basis, from other members of their own organisation, from customers and suppliers or from wider professional networks. Only a minority of respondents made frequent use of written or audio-visual materials like manuals, videos or computer-based training. The rest tried to circumvent materials by getting the information they needed from other people.

Formal education did play a role. Working for qualifications and short training courses were important for some people at particular stages in their career. Generally, initial training was judged better when it was both broad in scope and involved periods in the workplace as well as in the classroom, laboratory or workshop.

Chapter 5

Learning models, processes and practices

Chapter overview

- How people learn at work, what they learn and how useful and relevant this learning is – personally, for the enterprise and for the economy – is a relatively unresearched domain that poses both theoretical and practical challenges. We are now seeing the development of conceptual frameworks that acknowledge the complexity of learning in the workplace, providing a basis for good empirical research. Most of the literature in the field of learning and work has hitherto been concerned with training and training effectiveness, undertaken within a behaviourist, instructional paradigm. This research has been useful, and indeed as a result significant changes have taken place in the way training is designed and managed. Formal frameworks for learning typically fail when they neither address people's current concerns at work nor link to planned changes to which learners are already committed.

- Our understanding of workplace learning has greatly extended beyond the training paradigm, however. It is now seen in more multi-dimensional terms, informed by many different theoretical approaches. A valuable new perspective comes from recognition of the social, situated nature of much learning. The most useful studies for enlarging our understanding of just what is involved in learning at work, and how to foster a strong learning environment, are those which address this topic in a holistic or integrative way. There is still a place for focused research on particular learning processes, but these need to be contextualised by the broader picture. There is a danger that in abstracting, say, mentoring as an object of research inquiry we fail to see how inter-dependent this process of learning is with other features of the learning environment.

Conceptual models

Although coming to the domain of workplace learning from different starting points, there are marked similarities in the conceptual frameworks that researchers such as Onstenk, Eraut and colleagues, and a group at the Tavistock Institute have been developing on the basis of ongoing theorising and empirical research in this area.

The learning potential of jobs

Onstenk (1995b, 1997b) has an interest in what he terms 'the learning potential of jobs'. This refers to the likelihood that learning processes will occur in a particular job situation. It is dependent on:

- the available skills and learning abilities of the employee (that is, what they bring to the job and is shaped in other environments, notably education)

- the willingness of the employee to learn

- the learning opportunities on the job and in the workplace

- the availability of on-the-job training

- the relationships and mutual influences of these factors.

Learning processes which give rise to the development of competence (whether of knowledge, skill, understanding) result from the specific combination of the workers' skills and qualifications (formal education, work experience, learning skills), their ability and willingness to learn and develop competence, and the learning possibilities on the shop floor. The last of these, learning possibilities, is dependent on the characteristics of the job itself (scope and variety) and on the immediate work environment (its physical and social characteristics) (see Figure 2).

In earlier writing (1993), taking a wider human resource management approach, Onstenk's framework was extended to include aspects of the organisational environment which might, or might not, be conducive to the various dimensions of learning potential. Included here are such aspects of company policy and structure as career and personnel management, worker participation mechanisms and technology innovation, including in particular the use of information technologies.

Figure 2   The learning potential of jobs

Available skills	**Motivation to learn**
Educational level	Active motivation (learning attitude)
Work experience	
Core skills	Passive motivation (receptiveness)
Learning skills	

Learning possibilities	**Training on the job**
Job:	
Completeness	
Complexity	
Innovation, 'events'	Structuring learning opportunities
Problem-solving	
Planning	
Discretion space	
Social/work environment:	Participation in innovation
Colleagues, supervisors	
Feedback, explanations	
Information environment:	Structured training on the job
Information, computers	
Material clues	

(*Source*: Onstenk, 1995a,b)

Onstenk's model is intended as a framework for intervention in the context of organisational innovation and restructuring of the labour process. This would include, on the objective side, creating broader jobs where workers can develop multi-skilling through performing more tasks; fostering the exercise of autonomy through setting up small work groups with responsibility for solving problems on the work line; providing more opportunities for exchange and mutual learning; and shaping and changing the subjective dimension of learning potential, namely employees' willingness and ability for self-directed learning.

A learner-centred framework

Eraut and colleagues (1998) developed and refined their framework in the course of a major investigation into the nature of learning at work, undertaken as part of the UK ESRC Learning Society programme. Concerned to capture learning at work in all its forms, their study made no prior assumptions about the role of education and training. Rather, the interest was in discovering both what was learned, how it was learned and what facilitated or constrained learning at work. A summary of their framework appears below in Figure 3.

Figure 3   Learning at work

| **What is being learned?** |
| 1 Understanding |
| 2 Skills |
| 3 Propositional knowledge |
| 4 Knowledge resources and how to access them |
| 5 Judgement |

| **How is it being learned?** |
| 1 Working for qualifications |
| 2 Short courses |
| 3 Special events |
| 4 Materials |
| 5 Organised learning support |
| 6 Consultation and collaboration within the working group |
| 7 The challenge of the work itself |
| 8 Consultation outside the working group |
| 9 Life outside work |

| **Factors affecting learning** |
| Personal characteristics |
| 1 Confidence |
| 2 Motivation |
| 3 Capability/prior knowledge |
| The micro-context |
| 4 How a person is managed |
| 5 The micro-culture of the workplace |
| The macro-context |
| 6 The organisation |
| 7 Professional bodies |
| *(Source: Eraut et al, 1998)* |

The team of researchers found that using the framework helped them to find connections between what was learned at work and how it was learned. Locating the learner at the centre of their framework, rather than the provider or facilitator of learning, their empirical study provides insights into how learners make use of different learning contexts (formal courses, short courses, the work group, the challenge of work itself, consultation outside the immediate working group) to acquire different kinds of understanding, skills and knowledge.

The factors affecting learning (although not necessarily translating into improved performance) include:

- the personal characteristics of the learner (prior knowledge and capability, motivation and confidence)

- the micro-context of the workplace (how a person is managed and the micro-learning culture), and

- the macro-context of the organisation and external professional bodies.

The learning configuration

Researchers at the Tavistock Institute refer to 'learning configurations' (Tavistock Institute 1994, 1996). Originating out of research into the use of new learning technologies in work, educational and community settings, their conceptual framework sets out the different elements that need to be considered together when designing a system of learning. Effective learning occurs when there is congruence between the profile of the learners, the learners' needs and aspirations (learning content and skills), the learning paradigm (instruction or experiential, interaction patterns and group dynamics) and the delivery system (the way learning is managed, how learners are recruited, timing and pacing, etc). These elements come together in a learning scenario. But learning is also affected by wider considerations to do with the organisational setting, and beyond that the socio-economic and cultural environment.

The Tavistock work also draws attention to the economic dimension alongside the pedagogic, organisational and institutional aspects that figure in all three conceptual frameworks. This is a much neglected area of research into learning at work, although of great importance to employers. Some modes of learning are clearly more resource intensive than others and there are trade-offs to be made between pedagogic effectiveness and economic efficiency.

The value of these conceptual frameworks lies in their recognition of the interconnectedness between the different elements or components, and hence the essential contingent nature of learning and learning effectiveness. Some kinds of learning processes are heavily dependent on motivation and capabilities acquired prior to work. The effectiveness of others is contingent on the way work is organised; learning processes that are well matched to the learning styles of people at professional levels may not yield learning outcomes at lower levels of the organisation; lack of variation or challenge in a job lowers the rate of learning, while critical incidents or difficult problems can be a significant source of learning. All learning processes are affected by factors beyond the immediate working environment, from the micro-organisational climate extending out to national policies or wider socio-economic factors.

The learning environment

In the following sections, three key aspects of the workplace as a learning environment are addressed:

- the potential for learning that is built into the job and the immediate work task environment, ie *the challenge of work itself*

- the management and facilitation of learning, ie *the role of managers/key workers in supporting the learning process*

- the organisational context – policies, systems, structures, mechanisms, ie *creating a learning culture.*

The challenge of work itself

New ideas about workplace learning emphasise the potential for learning that is embedded within the work itself. One strand of research is concerned with the formation and development of skills through job design and the structuring of the learning experience on and through the job; the other focuses more on continuous learning work and the linking of learning with business initiatives and organisational changes. These two are brought together through a range of learning opportunities, from the least to the most structured activities or, in other words, from the most informal to the formal (see Figure 4).

Figure 4   The continuous learning continuum

Informal	Unanticipated experiences and encounters that result in learning as an incidental by-product, which may or may not be consciously recognised.
	New job assignments and participation in teams, or other job-related challenges that are used for learning and self-development.
	Self-initiated and self-planned experiences – including the use of media (print, television, radio, computers), seeking out a tutor or coach or mentor, attendance at conferences, travel or consulting.
	Total quality groups/action learning or other vehicles designed to promote continuous learning for continuous improvement.
	Planning a framework for learning, which is often associated with career plans, training and development plans, or performance evaluations.
	Combination of less organised experiences with structured opportunities, which may be facilitated, to examine and learn from those experiences.
	Designed programmes of mentoring and/or coaching, or of on-the-job training.
	Just-in-time courses, whether they are delivered as classes or through self-learning packages, with or without the assistance of technology.
	Formal training programmes
Formal	Formal programmes leading to a qualification.

Source: Adapted from Watkins and Marsick, 1993

Jobs differ greatly in content, complexity, variety and the degree of autonomy available to the worker. Lack of variation or lack of challenge lowers the rate of learning. Jobs that are learned quickly and then handled reactively by intuitive recognition of the situation and the application of a 'well-tested' solution similarly reduce the potential for ongoing learning. Raper et al (1997), for example, found that although garment manufacturers in the textile industry had introduced multi-skilling to increase flexibility, the work itself was repetitive and there was little else that a structured form of on-the-job learning could do to add value to the product.

Where maintenance tasks or quality control is integrated into the job, work groups have more scope to develop higher-level skills. New process technologies make demands on operators because of their interactive complexity and the many ways in which surprises can occur (Weick, 1990). Skills in monitoring and diagnostics are crucial, and people must be committed to do what is necessary on their own initiative and have the autonomy to do so, dealing with and counteracting the 'unexpected'. Thus, while many routine tasks are automated, non-routine tasks are left for human judgement, requiring tough decisions. Work problems become learning problems when existing solutions are not effective and new completely satisfactory ones do not yet exist (Onstenk, 1997b). On the other hand, in lean production models, learning may be restricted to a series of low-level short-cycle tasks that are quickly learned on the job through mere repetition. The quality of learning depends on the sequence of problems and 'critical events' (Zarifian, 1991) occurring in day-to day-work practice.

Continuous learning in the job can be planned intentionally, discovered serendipitously, absorbed incidentally, or revealed retrospectively (Watkins and Marsick, 1993). Research undertaken by Eraut et al (1998) among technical and professional staff revealed a number of ways in which such learning occurred:

- changes in work role and special assignments, which stimulated or necessitated new learning (typical examples were acting up, being 'on call', becoming a mentor, joining a review group)

- the initial period in a new job

- a difficult problem or critical incident

- changes in a person's duties and expectations about work processes or outcomes.

Those in leadership or management roles faced problems of a rather different kind. They still had a steady flow of critical incidents and problems hitting their desk, but they also had an ongoing challenge of a more strategic kind. They were expected to improve both the efficiency of their work unit and the quality of its work. This required them to prioritise, to innovate and to frame problems whose solution might lead to improved performance.

People can learn without paying much attention to what they are learning. There is a strong line of pedagogical thinking, however, which holds that to maximise the benefits of much (informal) workplace learning, people need to bring what they are learning into conscious awareness. They learn more effectively through a process of questioning, reflection and feedback from others that, permits deeper understanding to emerge from these otherwise everyday activities (Schon, 1983).

On the shop floor, such reflective activities may be built into team meetings, quality circles, problem-solving groups, continuous improvement groups and the like. In the service industries and among managerial groups, techniques such as action learning, scenario-building, research circles, experiential team learning, and cross-functional change team meetings are often found. These are sometimes facilitated by someone in a key worker role – whether team leader, supervisor or trainer. The Swedish Learning at Work innovation programme, in which 35 projects were conducted in major companies and public sector organisations, experimented with techniques such as learning dialogues, study circles, boundary crossing groups, mentoring and action learning. The work of Eraut et al also demonstrated that people often share experiences with colleagues and/or friends, and thus there is a significant amount of learning and reflection through peripheral participation. By the same token, learning can be initiated by another person offering feedback or advice about one's performance, one's role or even one's future prospects.

On-the-job training, to be effective as a method of skills formation and development, also needs to be built into a cycle of action and reflection. Onstenk (1995b) argues that structured on-the-job training should be a planned and managed process, involving a pedagogical structuring of progressively more difficult work tasks, supported by feedback, supervision and teaching aids. The use of work assignments, work-based projects, learning log associated with a portfolio, or oral presentations are methods for ensuring that systematic reflection occurs.

What seems to be evident from the above is that although learning can be informal and unplanned, it is more likely to be effective where there is some kind of organised learning support. The different forms that such support might take are discussed in the next section.

The facilitation of learning

The facilitation of learning in the workplace takes a variety of forms, dependent in part of the prevailing level of formality and structure in the workplace, and the initiator of the learning support. This may be the learner, the organisation (HRD department), the line manager or another (usually more experienced) colleague.

On the basis of their practical work in companies, Levy et al (1992) put forward a range of strategies grouped into four main areas that could be taken by line managers and supervisors in order to promote the learning of an individual worker-learner. These included:

- Moving the learner to different locations in the organisation to experience different parts of the work environment and to have an opportunity to observe or shadow particular personnel (a form of induction and job rotation).

- Sequencing the learner's activities and creating learning opportunities that would not otherwise occur (gradation of tasks, facilitating the progression from novice to expert).

- Changing the scope of learner activities through extending the discretion given to the learner, changing the extent and type of supervision and increasing or decreasing the range of activities engaged in by the learner.

- Fostering learner awareness of skill and performance through providing opportunities for feedback, debriefing and reflection, helping learners to analyse their activities and to be aware of the skills involved, and making explicit the competences and skills required in the learner's work role.

Structured learning of this kind is sometimes linked with an individual learning plan, and the results of the learning process are monitored and assessed by a supervisory or experienced colleague. Another approach involves giving rather complicated work assignments linked to different tasks (Onstenk, 1995b), use of Leittext methods (Schmidt-Hackenburg, 1992) or problem-oriented training which can be used to enrich the learning opportunities available in jobs or settings that are otherwise unpromising (Evans et al, 1987).

There is some consonance between this set of strategies and the approaches to the facilitation of learning identified by Eraut et al (1998) in their work with technical and professional groups in company settings. However, whereas Levy and colleagues were more concerned with new trainees and apprentices, the research group under Eraut was focused more on the continuous learning work of workers in established positions and roles.

The following four approaches were found to operate sometimes on their own and sometimes in combination:

Induction and integration

This focuses primarily on people becoming effective members of their work unit and of the organisation as a whole. The emphasis is on socialisation: understanding the purposes and goals of the unit and the organisation, their own roles and others' expectations of them; and fitting into the interpersonal nexus in which their work is embedded. The management approach can vary from *laissez-faire* and light monitoring to a succession of formal events, eg an induction course followed by other short courses. The way in which mentoring was used as a key method for socialisation of trainees in Marconi is described by Russell, 1994.

Exposure and osmosis

These terms are frequently used to describe the process of learning by 'peripheral participation' (Lave and Wenger, 1991). Through observations and listening, the learner picks up information and know-how by a process of osmosis. The role of the manager is limited to that of enabling sufficient exposure to a diversity of contexts and situations, but otherwise remains passive. The learner, on the other hand, has not only to be alert and receptive but also to work out what he or she needs to know. Shadowing and certain types of rotation and visit are the usual methods employed. The first three of Levy's strategies fit in here.

Self-directed learning

This assumes that the learner takes a more active role, learning from doing the work and finding out on their own initiative what they need to know. Such an active role is more likely to be adopted if the work is chosen appropriately and the learner encouraged in their learning. Like the first two approaches, managers' hopes that employees will be self-directed learners may not be realised if the attitude of the managers is perceived as less than positively supportive.

Structured personal support for learning

This involves the use of supervisors, mentors or coaches. Sometimes this is an official process; sometimes the role is assumed by a manager or a more experienced colleague; sometimes a manager asks someone to provide help and advice; sometimes the learner is encouraged to seek advice from a particular colleague or colleagues. Whether officially organised or not, the climate of the workplace is likely significantly to affect the quality of learning support.

A major factor affecting a person's learning at work was the personality, interpersonal skills, knowledge and learning orientation of their manager. Dankbaar (1995) argues that if workers in self-regulating groups 'are to be encouraged to be creative and make suggestions for technical and organisational improvements, they must be "empowered" and this requires that managers learn to share and delegate power, to trust and coach their personnel, instead of simply giving orders. The capacity of middle managers to adopt such attitudes has been over-estimated'. Eraut et al (1998) also found that most learning at work, where it happened, resulted from relatively informal inputs initiated by middle managers, colleagues or learners themselves. This has major implications for how managers and other key workers are best prepared for their role. This issue has been taken up by Brown et al (1994) in a study of the role of key workers.

The role of 'key worker' as facilitator of learning

The changes in organisations associated with delayering or flatter organisational hierarchies, which in some cases have also seen the abandonment of training departments, has increased the importance of the role for first line supervision. In many organisations, supervisors or other 'key workers' have assumed responsibility for identifying training needs, setting up training arrangements on the job, and evaluating effectiveness of training through monitoring standards of work.

In some companies, devolution of the training role has gone even further, with the group leader of a team assuming responsibility. In yet more participatory and working environments, each worker is a 'key worker', supporting and developing the skills and capabilities of others through the intertwining of learning and working activities. This latter approach depends not only upon a culture in which learning is valued, but also upon helping, supporting and training skills being effectively distributed very widely throughout the workforce.

The issues that surround the role of 'key workers' in the British enterprise were explored in case studies and a survey by Brown et al (1994). Variation in key worker roles, and the way in which they were developed and supported, was found to be contingent on the competitive strategy of the company, reflected in its skills strategy, mode of organisation, work structure and time horizon. The principal conclusions drawn from their research were:

- In organisations where a high level of skills and a high level of competitive market responsiveness is required, the *individual worker* is the key worker

- In other market sectors and types of organisation, the key worker as *trainer* may suffice

- For *all* types of organisation, the way forward lies in the development of key workers (whether work-based trainers, supervisory, or individual workers) as *working coaches*, able to help and support others.

This last point echoes strongly the conclusion reached by Eraut et al (1998) in their study of workplace learning. They likewise believe that of all the mechanisms used at organisational level to promote learning, the most significant is likely to be the appointment and development of its managers. 'However, while approaches to management development normally emphasise motivation, productivity and appraisal, comparatively little attention is given to supporting the learning or subordinates, allocating and organising work, and creating a climate which promotes informal learning.'

Among aspects of the key worker role explored by Brown et al (1994), were the factors that make for success in introducing and sustaining its three variants:

The trainer as 'key worker'

In some companies, trainers carried much of the responsibility for education and training, including developing teamwork and communication skills, as well as setting up mentoring schemes. In other cases, they were responsible for technical updating and encouraging staff to undertake external qualifications. Where they fulfilled clearly identified training needs and could plug into well developed structures (open learning centres, financial support for those undertaking qualifications) they could be effective up to a point. Problems often derived, however, from their separate function. They were not integrated into the management structure, and they sometimes suffered a 'credibility gap' in that they were encouraging 'ideal ways' which were countermanded by the exigencies of the 'real world' of production.

The supervisor as 'key worker'

In other companies changes in the organisation of work (for example, greater teamwork) or in the structure of the organisation (de-layering of middle management) meant that the supervisor was seen as the 'key worker'. The prospective roles and training needs of the supervisor varied widely. In some cases (for example, in the clothing industry), it was thought necessary to build up the technical skills of supervisory staff; whereas in other cases, technical skills were widely distributed throughout highly skilled teams, and emphasis was placed upon development of management and organisational skills. Some companies made internal selections and then used intensive training programmes, drawing on external educational support, whereas others sought a new type of recruit for the role. In many instances, the role of the supervisor was portrayed as being a 'facilitator;' who could communicate with, motivate and support others. The extent to which they were given explicit training and the opportunity to develop such 'soft' skills varied widely.

This model, Brown and colleagues suggest, is likely to be viable in a range of organisational contexts, typically when moves are made to get away from Fordist principles, but the 'normal' work tasks for many workers are still constrained.

This is likely to be the case in companies/sectors identified as having transitional organisational forms. The role of the supervisor too can be clearly focused upon production, but with recognition of the need for team development. However, the researchers see a danger that this model will be chosen when changing patterns of work organisation would make it more appropriate to devolve responsibility and control still further to workers as individuals and/or as members of teams.

The worker as ' key worker'

This third model of the key worker, whereby each individual worker is perceived as a key worker, was not well represented among the organisations surveyed by Brown et al. Indeed, it seems likely that the number of organisations for whom this model is most appropriate may still be relatively small. For example, they would have high-level skill requirements, flat organisational structures, and requirements for integrated teamwork. Such demands are likely to become more significant if organisations wish to be perceived as high skill, high quality and high value-added learning organisations.

In such a model, it is expected that the key worker would develop the coaching and support skills necessary to support the development of others through the intertwining of work and learning activities. Similarly, teams and groups of workers would arrange work and learning activities to meet their own planning, problem-solving and development needs.

The learning culture

The research literature, particularly that reporting on empirical studies, generally points up the obstacles and constraints in the way of moving towards or achieving a learning environment. While there is a vast literature, evangelical and prescriptive in nature, on the learning organisation, there is little by way of hard evidence on learning or performance outcomes.

Here, we confine ourselves to reviewing studies which have something to say about factors at the micro-level of the 'learning culture' in organisations and the kinds of organisational enabling structures that can facilitate or impede workplace learning. Mention is also made of one or two external factors in the wider environment which impinge on firms, notably the emergent policy discourse of 'employability' and the degree of co-operation between management and unions.

Schuck (1996) draws attention to the need to foster an environment of inquiry, in which people talk to each other, play with ideas and are able to recognise and use learning opportunities at work. Whether people respond to a workplace designed to support inquiry depends largely on the quality of social interactions and the attitudes of workers and managers. People must feel free and be eager to ask questions, to feel that their requests would be received positively, and must demonstrate a willingness to share their knowledge. The beliefs, attitudes and behaviours of the manager are crucial here. As Eraut et al (1998) concluded from their study, 'it follows that of all the mechanisms used at organisational level to promote learning, the most significant is likely to be the appointment and development of its managers'.

Why would some managers discourage workers from learning? Typically, managers are rewarded for their individual expertise, for having the answers. They are more often rewarded for possessing knowledge than for distributing it. Since knowledge is such an important resource in a learning organisation, we might expect much political activity to be associated with how it is acquired, and how access to it is controlled. Coopey (1996) has drawn attention to the way in which people who perceive themselves to be especially disadvantaged in the move towards a learning organisation may defend any erosion of their status and influence. This applies not only to managers, but also to workers, who may resist pressures for their tacit knowledge to be translated into objective collective knowledge which, potentially, others can use within the dialectic of control.

Pedler et al (1991) provide an example of the constraints that managerial prerogative places on employee discretion even within a learning organisation. In reviewing the implications of an extensive learning initiative in the Rover Car Group its then Chairman, Graham Day, is quoted as saying, 'We realise that by encouraging continuous learning and development among all our employees, they will start to question more and more the way we manage things. We will have to learn to respond appropriately to that, but we are not a democracy – the buck stops with management.'

Mentoring is often seen as an alternative way of providing coaching without the complication of line management responsibility (Russell, 1994). Through mentors, employees learn to take risks, communicate effectively, deal with the politics of the organisation and hone specific professional skills. Zey (1984) elaborates on some of the techniques involved in this kind of learning: non-directive teaching that enhances independence and self-confidence, Socratic questioning, learning by doing under supervision, and role participation that allows the protégé to question him or her on the rationale for actions.

Skruber (1987) highlights the importance of a learning climate or culture that encourages, rewards and provides mechanisms for learning. Barriers in the culture include the need to be right every time, a tendency not to admit mistakes and therefore not to learn from them, and a feeling that formal classroom learning is the only way to acquire new skills and knowledge. Cultures of this kind can exercise a strong formative influence within industry sectors and professional groupings. An EU pilot study investigating the potential for just-in-time learning in the banking sector attributed the poor take-up of the new learning technology by individual employees to the dominant culture in banks which militates against acknowledging mistakes or having insufficient knowledge about a product (Articulate, 1995).

Individual readiness for work

Marsick (1987) identifies 'individual readiness' for learning at work as an important issue. Continuous learning work depends on increased participation of all individuals in decision-making and in dialogue about shared goals, norms, values and procedures. Central to this new mode of learning and working on an individual level are autonomy, initiative, independent judgement, self-direction and a reservoir of experience and knowledge appropriate to the tasks being faced. Many workers are quite happy with jobs that are clearly defined and that do not require ongoing reflection. Reflection, whether simple or critical, requires personal change that might not be desired by the individual or desirable in many organisational contexts, given the concern of both the company and the workers for maximising profits.

Continuous learning can be enhanced when people are proactive, reflective and creative in their learning. Learning may start as a reaction to events, but proactive individuals quickly take charge of their learning. For a variety of reasons, however, substantial sectors of the workplace may not have such a positive orientation towards learning nor the skills and capacities that would allow them to exploit the learning opportunities available in their workplace. While this may reinforce a belief on the part of many managements that their staff 'are incapable of thought' (James, 1991), research studies suggest that lower-level workers are often ready for greater levels of autonomy than they typically exercise and want to learn how to participate more fully in decision-making relevant to their own jobs (Munnelly, 1987). Ravid's (1987) study of self-directed learning indicates that such workers might be ready for this kind of autonomy in learning as well, although they may not be as accustomed to setting their own goals, identifying alternative ways of learning and resources, and monitoring their own progress.

Many mechanisms or techniques that have been introduced by human resource development departments to support continuous learning in the workplace are based on the expectation that people are motivated and skilled enough to be self-directed learners. Self-directed learning should not be difficult for employees who already know how to set realistic goals for themselves, can deal with the ambiguity involved when learning assignments are not structured for them, can plan activities to reach their goal, and can continually assess their progress and revise their goals (Watkins and Marsick, 1993). Many employees do not already have these skills. Learning plans and individual professional development plans may not be sufficient because people do not know enough about what they need, the way they learn or how to enhance their skills.

These difficulties have been addressed in some companies through a greater degree of structured guidance, with assistance from self-identified supervisors, colleagues, and specialists such as trainers or career counsellors.

Various mechanisms and strategies have been adopted by companies as part of a 'whole of company' approach to workforce learning. These include:

- employee development schemes, providing opportunities to develop basic skills that were not acquired in the education system as well as a general 'learning how to learn' capability and a more positive attitude towards learning

- developmental learning plans

- the use of professional learning guidance/counsellors

- learning maps that help employees plan for their own learning and give the organisation a way to monitor activities that are otherwise hard to monitor, evaluate and explain to higher levels of management

- establishment of open learning centres.

Learning plans or individual professional plans, disassociated from performance appraisal systems or other mechanisms for career development, are favoured by many companies as a kind of steering mechanism for learning. Such plans cover short- and long-term learning goals and include realistic strategies to achieve goals and specify the combination of people, activities, mentoring and coaching, job assignments and other resources to achieve goals. Some plans also emphasise strategies to obtain feedback necessary for self-assessment and reshaping of goals.

Evaluation of employee development schemes has pointed to the importance of independent learning advisers, located in open learning centres, as a critical factor in raising participation levels and delivering learning outcomes (Toronto, 1993; Forrester et al, 1993).

Putting an open learning centre in place is no guarantee that employees will use it or that either party will benefit from it. There appears to be a general expectation that employees will be sufficiently motivated to enhance their skills and competences in their own time. The employee response across a range of organisations included in the Tavistock Institute (1998a) research seems to be that they welcome such a centre on site, but that they do not have time to use it after work because they are either too tired from shift work, or they have other commitments outside work. In a number of organisations the researchers found that employees at the operative or clerical level were not even aware that such a centre existed. More significantly, in a number of cases employees refused to use their own time for developing work-related knowledge and skills. They regarded training as something that should be built into their working time.

Organisation enabling structures and obstacles

Many companies lack the types of sophisticated personnel management systems necessary to make effective training and utilisation of workers' abilities a reality. A substantial body of literature has drawn attention to the lack of an integrated approach to human resource management and subsequent 'weak' representation of personnel and training departments; devolution of responsibility to line managers (who, caught between conflicting rationales, tend to overlook training issues); managers who are themselves poorly educated; and the perennial fear of 'poaching' felt by many employers (Legge, 1995; Keenoy, 1990; Rainbird, 1994; Sisson and Storey, 1993).

The existing managerial performance systems in the UK are still very much geared towards the achievement of short-term financial/accounting targets, including a constant quest for labour-related cost reduction.

To talk of careers, in any meaningful sense, is for many employees to ignore reality. For the majority of process and non-craft skilled workers in many sections of manufacturing industry, for example, well-formed internal labour markets and job security are often lacking, while opportunities for progression are minimal with the current employer and limited within the sector as a whole. In the clothing industry, for example, the recent situation was that 'a typical female machinist enters the industry in her early 20s and retires from the industry maybe 40 years later – as a machinist' (Bosworth et al, 1990). Retailing, cleaning, distribution, hotel and catering, food and tobacco, clothing and textiles, and leisure and tourism are examples of sectors where well developed internal labour markets and career structures frequently do not exist. These sectors employ a significant proportion of the national workforce (Brown et al, 1994).

With the possible exception of degree-level education, there is very scant evidence that British pay and reward structures are able to provide substantial incentives to the individual to acquire skills. Research by Bennett et al (1992) shows that many young people are quite rational in not pursuing training – it does not give them great enough reward. In many UK enterprises, 'pay and status are rarely linked to the attainment of qualifications and to attendance at training courses, so they provide little incentive to British employees to seek further training' (Coopers and Lybrand Associates, 1985). Moreover, a significant proportion of firms offer their employees extremely limited opportunity for progression.

Brown et al (1994) have also drawn attention to organisational obstacles in the way of developing coaching expertise in key workers. Despite the positive intentions, difficulties were encountered in the three companies studied which undermined the success of the coaching role and the importance attached to developing coaching expertise:

- The companies were not able to accommodate the numbers within internal progression routes.

- The development of coaching expertise was little regarded for career advancement purposes and neither was it seen as an important activity by many staff because of the way work itself was organised.

- The decision to undertake qualifications was seen as reflecting an individual decision to gain further qualifications, rather than seeing this particular qualification as strategically important.

- Those employers who offered support tended to do so as a generalised commitment to training rather than coaching itself being identified as critical.

Lack of reward incentives also appears to be an obstacle to effective team working and the broadening of skills. One of the findings from the study by Brown et al. (1994) was that team working generally took a long time to build up and to be successful; team members had to show interest in learning how to do other jobs within the unit. This could be difficult when the team was composed of people at different grades. There was no incentive for someone being paid at a higher level to learn to do the work of a less well-paid employee. By the same token, with the new flatter organisation and with reduced staffing levels, there was no incentive for the better-paid employee to increase his/her range of skills because there was little immediate opportunity for promotion. Onstenk (1997b) similarly notes that the optimal use of small work groups and multi-skilled groups implies job security, long-term contracts for the core staff and clear career paths. But many classification and pay systems are not adequately geared to working in groups, and the loss of supervisory jobs in delayering can lead to a break in traditional career paths for production jobs.

Organisational restructuring

The association of new approaches to workplace learning with organisational restructuring, including delayering, has meant that in many cases the reduction of the workforce has coincided with the time that the market model and a related 'empowerment' ethos was introduced. Not surprisingly, this was associated with resistance to change (Tavistock Institute, 1998a; Eraut et al, 1998).

Continuous improvement, seen by some as coupled with continuous learning work, is attracting more critical attention. Evidence at both theoretical and empirical levels abounds as to the inimical effects that can accompany the adoption of just-in-time and TQM approaches. Far from the ideals of emancipation and empowerment promised by democratic Taylorism, issues such as surveillance and monitoring, work intensification, internalisation of market conditions, etc are frequently mentioned and need to be further explored (see for example, Tuckman, 1994; Sewell and Wilkinson, 1992; Dawson and Webb, 1989).

New policy discourse

Quite a new factor that figures prominently in management and company discourse in the UK is that of employability, with the Government and employers stressing that as there is no security of employment any more, both the employer and the employee him/herself have the responsibility for his/her employability. This new discourse opens the way for a different 'contract' with employees whereby employers make a commitment to enhance the employability of their staff by providing mainly work-related CVT and by setting up a 'training infrastructure', and in return employees accept the lack of any guarantee for lifetime employment and try to remain 'employable' by making use of existing training opportunities and facilities. The 'employability' rationale, observed by the Tavistock Institute (1998a) in research with UK organisations, ultimately devolves responsibility for training and learning to the individual. In the absence of support mechanisms such as career guidance, personal development plans and the availability of facilitators within learning centres, this all too readily becomes a further extension of the 'great training robbery'. A quote from one of their case study interviews well exemplifies the managerial attitude as regards employability:

> I believe that people should drive their own training and development. That's the one single thing I say to everyone who comes into contact with me.... because if you don't believe you are getting the training and development that you need, whose problem is it really....I mean I am on this real purge, to try and transfer the accountability for training and development on to the individual.

Co-operative industrial relations is widely perceived to be an important factor in creating a receptive climate for learning. Managers are generally more likely to invest in workers' skills if there is a strong voice representing the interests of employees, and organised labour is supportive of the other changes such as new technologies and flexible job definitions. The UK's relatively weak and often adversarial trade unions do not usually encourage managers to adopt high skills work organisations. Changes such as the broadening of job classifications which have the potential to increase the capabilities of their members have been opposed by some unions as likely to reduce their power and accord management too much arbitrary discretion (Mason et al, 1994). There are exceptions to this pattern, notably the employee development schemes that conform to the 'personal developer' model described by Forrester et al (1993) with joint employer/union involvement, although even here significant obstacles were encountered to the effective use of learning centres set up under the scheme.

Formal and informal reward systems can also be obstacles to workplace learning. Peer pressure against norm-busting is a well recognised phenomenon in Taylorist regimes, but it can take on a new form in contemporary IT company environments. Schuck (1996) reports from her studies in companies that the issue is no longer how much you do but 'how much you think'.

Chapter 6

Workplace learning and performance improvement

Chapter overview

- Does workplace learning pay off, or is investing in the professional development of the workforce more a value-based decision than a business one? Employers have generally considered training as a cost rather than an investment, and the difficulties of establishing the direct links between investing in human capital and business success do little to encourage a change of perception among employers about the benefits of workplace learning.

- Performance effectiveness is not just about business success, however, as many employers attest. There is interest in knowing what kinds of learning methods, processes and activities are effective in producing different learning outcomes, and whether investment in human resource development of the company as a whole enhances organisational performance, and indeed the quality of working life of individual employees.

- This chapter pulls together disparate studies which provide evidence for a linkage between workplace learning and performance improvement, although the relationship is often indirect and relates to outcomes that may be a long way back in the chain from the final productivity and financial effects sought by many.

- A more critical perspective would challenge the very notion of 'performance' as it is currently understood and interpreted in the HR management literature. It is grounded in a training paradigm that is largely built on a 'skills deficit' model, and in a particular view of organisations. Many of today's learning problems are embedded in complex personal, social and organisational habits that are not amenable to training solutions. Employees also need to rethink their relationship to productive enterprise and thus to one another as partners in this enterprise. It is instructive that the two key variables in accounting for business success that emerged from analysis of the US Educational Quality of the Workforce National Employers Survey were:

  - practices that encouraged workers how to think and interact to improve the production process

  - unionised plants that had adopted such practices as employee participation.

A framework for linking workplace learning and performance improvement

The development of human capital, and its contribution to business success and the economy more generally, has long been a topic of debate and controversy. Reviewing the state of the debate, Woodhall (1997) concludes that 'the concept of investment in human capital is still valid, but it must be extended to include activities which affect personal attributes as well as skills, and it must recognise that such activities increase workers' productivity in complex ways'.

Keep and Mayhew (1994) echo this theme in arguing that 'although fairly simplistic attempts to read across from investment in training to business performance have been made... the evidence indicates that the linkages are complex and indirect. The research that is able to demonstrate such a linkage is generally based on case studies, from which it is hazardous to generalise.'

The characteristics that distinguish workplace learning from training make the task of assessing the effectiveness of learning at work even more daunting. In a review of research on learning and work undertaken for OECD, Raizen (1994) remarked that little is known about either the promotion or the effectiveness of on-the-job learning or job-specific skills. Although there is a burgeoning literature on non-formal and informal learning processes, there are very few studies of what is happening on the shop floor and these are rarely linked to performance outcomes. Finegold and Levine (1997) suggest that measures of on-the-job learning will be taken more seriously if they have been shown to predict important outcomes.

Nonetheless, it is possible to create a framework that allows us to map some of the accumulating evidence about linkages between workplace learning and performance improvement while being mindful of the tentative nature of the conclusions that can be drawn. Such a framework requires the development of a spectrum of outcome measures for increasingly remote effects of learning, as outlined in Figure 5 opposite. Some measures are subjective, others have a more objective basis. Employee commitment, for example, might be gauged from self-reports by employees or perceptions of employers, while absenteeism rates and turnover of labour stand as quantifiable 'proxy' measures for performance at the level of the enterprise.

While a great deal of research has addressed the effectiveness of instruction-based training in respect of these different variables, the benefits of more experiential on-the-job kinds of training and learning are far more difficult to establish. This has partly to do with the open-ended, situated nature of workplace learning in comparison with training, which is time and spatially bounded and where the effects of training can be assessed at the end or shortly after a training activity. On-the-job learning, in contrast, is a more fluid and continuous process, often lacking an explicit pedagogy and statement of learning outcomes. Performance improvement may be demonstrated more by the development of expertise than the achievement of threshold standards of skill competence (Onstenk, 1998 pers comm).

Moreover, the benefits or outcomes from workplace learning are often inseparable from the benefits of the work reorganisation and other personnel management initiatives. Let us take the Rover Car Company as an example. It spends £30 million

Figure 5   Outcome measures of performance effectiveness

Worker reactions	Individual variables
• reactions to training/learning experience • actual take-up of training/learning opportunities • reactions to HR strategies aimed at improving the quality of the workplace	
skills mastered, knowledge acquired, confidence improved	
changes in task performance and job behaviour	
job satisfaction increased motivation and commitment absenteeism and turnover	organisational variables (quality of working life)
changes in productivity and competitiveness efficiency of public sector organisations	business performance
profitability of the enterprise earnings profiles of individuals	financial effects

each year on learning and development. While not being able to measure the impact of the investment directly, the company points to business gains in the way of shareholder value, profitability and revenue per car sold, all of which have shown a dramatic improvement. The same is true of revenue per employee, breakdown levels and vehicle pipedown stocks. Business success is also evidenced by sales growth and customer satisfaction levels. However, Rover Learning Business is only one of nine key processes that drive the company. Others include new product introduction, product improvement, sales and service, and maintenance. Improved performance is more likely to be the outcome of an interrelated set of HRM, organisational design and business processes than any of these on their own (Sommerlad, 1996).

What does research tell us about the relationship between workplace learning and performance improvement, with respect to each of the main outcome measures identified above? Various studies have addressed this relationship, most of them concerned with only one or two links in this complex chain. Despite the limitations of a narrow focus, a number have explored new terrain in workplace learning and challenged some of the conventional assumptions about how people learn and what kinds of learning opportunities are best suited to the development of which kinds of knowledge, skills and understanding. One or two studies, such as the recent evaluation of the Investors in People initiative (Hillage and Moralee, 1996) have addressed a broader set of outcome measures, as well as having the benefit of a large sample of companies for teasing out relationships that are statistically significant. The relevance of this study lies in the serious commitment of Investors in People companies to the development of human resources. If there is an association to be found at the broadest level between investment in human resource development and performance improvement, then one would expect it to be manifest among the self-selecting group of IIP companies. Some substantiation for this belief comes from studies that have shown that companies with above average implementation of total quality programmes performed better financially

(Jarrell and Easton, 1994), while similar results were found for companies that won quality awards (Hendricks and Singhal, 1994). These companies tended to train more, and to integrate new skills into the workplace.

Worker reactions, skill development and task/job performance

The evaluation of training activities has typically had a 'before and after' focus, involving the gathering of information on participants' reactions to the training experience and a later follow-up on the usefulness of training in the real work environment. A main thrust of recent reform in company training has been the effort to link training more closely with the strategic business intent of the organisation and to adopt pedagogic strategies that enhance the prospects for transfer from the training environment to the workplace. This is sometimes expressed as a shift from decontextualised to contextualised training. It might involve, for example, the adoption of techniques such as 'learning assignments' that relate to problem-solving, task-centred activities and other targets as specified in the business plan.

Employee development schemes are interesting because many of them stand outside this shift towards contextualised learning, with a focus on the development of generic educational skills. Although newer kinds of pedagogy attempt to bridge this gulf by teaching basic skills in a highly contextualised way (Raizen, 1994; Engerstrom, 1994) so that the prospects for learning transfer are enhanced, much of the thinking behind open learning centres and encouragement for learning is unconcerned with its application and relevance. It is part of creating a more positive attitude towards learning, fostering employee motivation and commitment, and building a learning culture in the workplace. Evaluators of the employee development schemes in the UK commented that not enough is known about the relationship between generic educational skills and generic employment skills even to design an evaluation scheme which relates ED directly to the requirements of industry (Forrester et al, 1995b).

It is not the intention here to review the voluminous literature on training effectiveness that is situated within an instructional paradigm. Rather, our focus is confined to the findings from a small number of studies that address learning of a non-formal kind which are experience-led or which require self-direction on the part of the learner. Studies on worker reactions to various modes of workplace learning is a very weak indicator or outcome measure of performance improvement. At the most general level, the findings tell us something about the acceptability of different kinds of learning and training provision. This can be useful where new learning practices are involved, such as on-line or just-in-time learning. More relevant are studies which explore the connections between what is learned at work and how it is learned, in the context of the workplace itself rather than in a training setting. These tell us something about the contingent nature of workplace learning: some modes of learning are more appropriate for acquiring certain kinds of skills or knowledge than are others.

The study by Eraut et al (1998) on the development of knowledge and skills in employment takes such a grounded approach. The researchers found that the two modes of non-formal learning reported as important by nearly all respondents (in technical and professional roles) were learning from the challenge of the work itself, and learning from other people. Other kinds of learning that typically feature in company workplace training strategies, such as packaged open learning materials, manuals, journals and reference books, were perceived to be less relevant or useful. Packaged training, in particular, reinforced the image of a distant uncaring employer and was generally considered demotivating; manuals, reference books and materials linked to formal qualifications from professional bodies were welcomed but usage was confined to a minority who thrived on learning in this way.

A similar pattern of findings emerged from a much earlier study in the Honeywell company. Zemke (1985) found that 50 per cent of the ways in which managers learn to manage came from challenging job experiences, 30 per cent from relationships with others in the organisation, and only 20 per cent from training. While important, training was helpful primarily when it was specifically timed to meet pressing job demands and because it increased the development of collegial relationships. Relationships with both subordinates and supervisors were highly important to developing competence, as was responsibility for new or struggling projects and coaching. Obstacles on the job were seen as developmental rather than as setbacks, while hindrances included insufficient time for personal development, and superiors who emphasise short-term results.

The findings from these two studies are strongly supported by an increasingly large volume of literature which all points to the crucial importance of the social basis of learning (Frade, 1995).

Although the companies studied by Eraut et al provided training and further qualifications-based education, this mode of formal learning contributed to only a small proportion of learning at work. Formal propositional knowledge such as specialised occupational knowledge, firm specific knowledge or knowledge of systems and procedures, was often acquired as the result of substantial formal input. Non-formal learning, however, was important in developing the capability to use that knowledge at work. The contribution of formal learning to skills acquisition and development varied according to skill, the learning opportunities, and the learner's personal disposition. Most respondents expected some formal training in technical skills, but some insisted on learning by doing, with informal feedback. Changes in work role and special assignments stimulated or necessitated new learning. Typical examples were acting up, being 'on call', becoming a mentor, joining a review or policy-making group, or changes in a person's duties.

The Investors in People evaluation (Hillage and Moralee, 1996) included an employee survey aimed at eliciting workers' views of the benefits of IIP on the workplace as a whole, and their performance in the workplace. Overall, the results showed that most employees felt that the IIP process had left their workplace untouched. Those who did notice a positive effect, however, were more likely to be the lower-graded and lower-paid employees.

The nearly 2,000 companies sampled in the survey identified a number of improvements in performance which they attributed to their participation in the initiative. These were in the main areas of:

- employees' understanding of the business

- employees' skills and competences

- employee commitment

- employee communication.

There was a size effect here:

- Improvements in employees' understanding of the business were more important in smaller organisations (especially those with between 10 and 49 employees) than among larger concerns.

- Improvements to the skills and competence of the workforce were more likely to be identified by larger employers (with over 200 employees).

- Improved employee commitment and communications were also benefits noticed more by larger employers than by smaller ones.

One of the few studies looking at on-the-job learning (as a substitute for training) and task performance is reported by Weiss (1994). In his study of learning-by-doing by newly hired workers in a large US telecommunications manufacturer, Weiss found compelling evidence of large improvements in the productivity of workers in their first few months. However, there was no net change in their productivity after that, although the industry was experiencing rapid productivity growth – from other sources. The combined productivity growth from favourable changes in the composition of the workforce (quitting by the least productive new hires) and the growing competence of the remaining workers was 44 percent comparing two months' with one month's job experience. Weiss points out that the complete halt in productivity improvement after the first few months may arise from peer pressure. In some European countries this would be institutionalised through trade union agreements. More fundamentally, work organisation in this case was fixed, ie three different types of assembly plant operation with no direct link between pay and output for experienced workers.

The Weiss study was limited to semi-skilled production workers, with the advantage of using direct output measures instead of a proxy. The learning in question was relatively straightforward skill acquisition, situated within an essentially Taylorist production regime. It was closed-ended in the sense of having an explicit objective, ie to bring each new recruit up to carefully measured experienced-worker standard. The study was thus limited to the initial learning curve in a learning-poor job.

Quality of working life

The findings from three studies reviewed as part of this report provide some evidence for an association between workplace training and the quality of working life.

Employers participating in the Investors in People initiative expected a wide range of benefits from introducing the quality standards, frameworks, HR planning mechanisms and procedures associated with the initiative. In particular, they looked to the initiative to help them improve the skills and quality of their workforce, and increase staff motivation and morale. While the evaluation demonstrated that IIP has a major effect on the approach to managing people in employing organisations, it appears that this effect is largely qualitative. IIP influences an organisation's culture and its management style, as much as changing measurable processes. It therefore takes time for the full effect of the initiative to take hold and to feed through to overall organisational performance. At that point, there are many other influences, of which IIP is unlikely to be the most important.

Two-thirds of employers involved said that the improvements they had expected in terms of skills, motivation and workplace relationships had actually been achieved. Smaller employers were more positive than larger ones. However, between 60 and 70 per cent of respondents felt they could have realised these workforce benefits through other means.

The evaluators of the Investors initiative undertook their own research aimed at tracing the impact of the iniative on workforce performance more directly. The three indicators investigated were:

- absence (as measured by an organisation's average number of days sickness absence per head)

- labour turnover (as measured by voluntary resignations as a percentage of the current workforce)

- the existence of skill shortages (as measured by the existence of any hard-to-fill vacancies during the previous year).

On the first indicator, the results showed declining levels of absence as the effect of IIP materialises over time. However, absence levels remained higher than those found in non-participating control groups. On the second indicator, there was no differential effect that could attributed to participation in the initiative. Finally, on the third indicator, the data suggested there is an association between involvement in IIP and declining skill shortages.

Among the companies surveyed as part of the evaluation of employee development schemes, 52 per cent of employers registered an improvement in industrial relations as a result of the implementation, 23 per cent saw no change, and 23 per cent did not comment (Forrester et al, 1993).

The Canadian Workforce Training Survey identified a number of areas where benefits were reported by trainees who had undergone formal training. The highest ranked advantages, especially for women, were 'intangibles' – increased self-confidence, greater employability, improved job performance and increased job satisfaction. The analysis also found positive outcomes for firms that trained. Organisations with training programmes had more favourable performance trends than non-trainers in a number of areas including revenues, profitability, employee relations, quality, and productivity and their business viability and outlook.

Changes in business performance

A number of studies, each of a very different character, provide insights into the complex nature of the relationship between workplace learning, other intermediary processes such as organisational design and worker-manager relations, and performance effectiveness as measured by business performance.

In a multi-year study of steel finishing lines, companies with high levels of training, frequent worker–management discussions, many problem-solving teams, pay based on team productivity, and policies to avoid lay-offs had lines that ran 98 per cent of the time. Plants with none of these practices had only 88 per cent uptime, and also produced lower quality than did high-performance plants (Ichiniowski et al, 1994).

Using data from the 1994 US Educational Quality of the Workforce National Employers Survey, Black and Lynch (1997) found that what is associated with higher productivity is not so much whether or not an employer adopts a particular work practice, but rather how that work practice is actually implemented within the company. They also found that some practices that companies have adopted to increase productivity have had no impact. For example, neither total quality management nor profit-sharing exclusively for managers increased productivity (although profit-sharing for non-management workers did increase productivity). Unionised plants with traditional manager-worker reactions had a mixed impact on productivity; unionised plants that had adopted new workplace practices such as incentive-based compensation and employee participation were not only more productive than their old-fashioned unionised peers, but also outperformed non-union plants that had adopted similar new workplace practices. In sum, practices that encourage workers how to think and interact to improve the production process are strongly linked to increased productivity.

Case studies carried out by the Centre for the Development of Vocational Training (CEDEFOP) as part of its wide-ranging study on workplace learning in EU member countries (Mehaut and Delcourt, 1994) indicated something of the complexities of the relationship between experiential modes of workplace learning and work reorganisation. Many reorganised firms were success stories in terms of increased productivity but not necessarily in terms of workforce skill development. Both training and experience were making workers more understanding of process and product. This new learning was not merely accompanying change – it was helping to shake up the organisation. It was non-formal learning, not instruction-led training, that was 'assuming a strategic position in dealing with uncertainty'.

A micro-level study offers a comparative perspective on two car manufacturing plants, each taking a very different view of the kind of organisational design that would support continuous improvement and performance effectiveness, while maintaining worker morale. The study offers good insights into the complex nature of the relationships between learning, work organisation and business performance, and questions some of the assumptions commonly made about the advantages of human-centred design over Japanese-inspired 'lean production' models (Adler and Cole, 1993).

The researchers compared the Toyota GM joint venture NUMMI plant in the US, which follows a 'democratic Taylorism' model, with Volvo's Uddevalla plant which has been called a human-centred model. A key finding was that although the Uddevalla approach promised a higher potential for individual learning, NUMMI was the more effective model for organisational learning. In fact, it was the way these two were linked in the NUMMI plant which accounted for its significantly higher growth rate for productivity and manufacturing quality. Moreover, the researchers found no evidence to support the critique of the more Taylorist work design that its lack of opportunities for personal development and its regimentation would undercut worker motivation. Rather, the findings showed

that the discipline created by the job design creates not only world-class performance but also a highly motivating work environment. A more detailed account of the research study is provided below.

A tale of two auto plants

The Toyota GM NUMMI and the Volvo Uddevalla plants are similar in several important respects. They are both committed to treating employees as their most important assets and to providing opportunities for employee growth. The two organisations put great stock in worker training, although NUMMI offers no pay premium for the accumulation of new skills, while at Uddevalla team members' pay increases with the accumulation of demonstrated expertise. In both plants, there is a relatively strong partnership between union and management. Finally, they are both organised around production teams.

The internal organisations are different, however. At NUMMI, teams are composed of four or five workers under a team leader, and both team members and team leaders are hourly workers. Each team member performs a work cycle of about 60 seconds. In the final assembly department, the teams are linked in series, in a traditional 'Fordist' assembly line. Teams take on responsibility for quality assurance, preventive maintenance and internal job rotation schedules.

In the newly designed plant at Uddevalla, there is a less regimented environment, more task variety, more autonomy and a lot more team self-management. Each of eight production teams takes full responsibility for assembling the vehicle from the subsystem up – a work cycle of about two hours. The teams are large – 10 people as opposed to four or five at NUMMI – and they have much broader responsibilities. Not only do teams decide rotation schedules, they also do their own hiring and decide on their own overtime schedules. Teams elect their own leaders and often rotate the role.

Data on performance results reveal significant differences between the two plants. Both on productivity and quality of working life indicators, the NUMMI plant performed at a significantly higher level than the Uddevalla plant. This was manifest in:

- NUMMI productivity levels well above the US auto industry standard and higher than any other GM plant, with an average of 20.8 hours per vehicle, compared with an average of 40 hours to assemble a vehicle at Uddevalla

- greater efficiency and quality in the Toyota plant as measured by output, numbers of line breakdowns and inventory stockpiles

- low/steady absenteeism rate (3 per cent) at Toyota, in comparison with a high (22 per cent) combined rate of absenteeism and long-term disability at Volvo (reflecting also the high standing Swedish tradition of absenteeism)

- similar levels of staff turnover

Their research suggests that the primary factor explaining NUMMI's productive superiority is the company's effort constantly to improve the details of the production process. Workers at both plants were encouraged to seek out improvements, and all received feedback on their task performance over the respective work cycles. But at NUMMI, the workcycle is about 60 seconds long, performance of the cycle is very standardised, and it is easy to identify problems, define improvement opportunities and implement improved processes. At Uddevalla, the cycle was some two hours long, they had to track their task performance at a more detailed level, and the craft model of work organisation encouraged workers to believe they should have considerable latitude in how they performed each cycle. Although Uddevalla had a bonus system that encouraged work teams to improve performance continually, the team had neither the focus on the kinds of kaizen opportunities that drive NUMMI performance (because of Uddevalla's long work cycle) nor the tools to capture these opportunities (because they lacked standardised work practices).

The research findings also led the researchers to challenge the widely held assumption that world-class performance can be based on only very high intrinsic work satisfaction. The NUMMI experience indicated that even when work has a basically instrumental function for workers, it can be organised to sustain both a moderately high level of work motivation and world-class performance.

Finally, the study demonstrates the need to build explicit links between individual and organisational learning, rather than assuming that an increase in individual learning leads to an increase in organisational learning. Uddevalla designed an extremely impressive range of personal learning opportunities for its employees – induction, development of basic skills, on-the-job training, teacher and team spokesperson competences, and skills in other managerial and engineering areas. But this emphasis on individual learning had no counterpart in organisational learning. Little thought was given to how work groups might learn from one another to facilitate continuous improvement. Instead, all the emphasis was on job enlargement and job enrichment.

At NUMMI, standardisation was the key to stimulate improvement. The skill development strategies for individual workers are managed as a component of this process, rather than as a way of maximising personal opportunities. As a result, training focuses on developing deeper knowledge, not only of the relatively narrow jobs but also of the logic of the production system, statistical control process and problem-solving processes. Understanding a broader range of jobs is recognised as an important stimulus to kaizen efforts, but this broadening of skill builds on, rather than replaces, the standardised work processes and the deepening of skills.

Source: Adler and Cole, 1993

Financial improvement

Improved financial performance was not a primary motivation for employers seeking to be an Investor in People. Fewer employers identified financial performance as a benefit they were looking to gain from IIP, other than those who were looking for training or workforce benefits. Of those who did, less than half said that their expected benefits had been achieved, and 80 per cent of those said they could have been achieved by other means. However, 40 per cent of employers who said that the training or workforce objectives they sought from Investors had been realised felt that there was a flow through to financial performance.

In general, the workforce and training benefits that employers do see realised are a means to the end of building a more effective organisation. It is likely that the results reflect the fact that many employers do not see a direct link between IIP and financial performance, rather than that they do not think there is one at all.

> We hoped it would be advantageous, although we didn't expect a direct commercial benefit. We believed that better training would result in a better bottom line. It meant people would be more effective in their jobs, with a better understanding and know why things are done. Mistakes happen when people can't be bothered, not because they do not know how to do something. Therefore it is not just a training problem. – Small metal manufacturing company.
>
> (Hillage and Moralee, 1996)

Multiple regression analysis indicated that being a recognised Investor in People was positively related to profitability, but the finding was not statistically significant. Investment in training (ie training expenditure) was the only significant influence on profitability per employee, with increased expenditure on training leading to increased profitability – a finding consistent with other studies.

The Canadian Workforce Training Survey identified a number of areas where training had made an impact, bringing benefits to both employees and employers.

Employees who had received formal training benefited in terms of significant wage gains. After controlling for individual and establishment characteristics, the wage premium received by workers who had undertaken formal training with their current employer was in the order of 10 per cent. An additional premium was associated with training received from previous employers.

The analysis also found positive outcomes for firms that trained. Organisations with training programmes had more favourable performance trends than non-trainers in a number of areas including revenues, profitability, employee relations, quality, and productivity and their business viability and outlook.

Concluding comment

In sum, the evidence linking workplace learning and performance improvement is tenuous. The reasons for this are many and complex. They have to do with the elusive nature of much workplace learning, the inadequacy of conceptual frameworks for comprehending what 'performance' outcomes might be in a modern enterprise, the paucity of 'fine grained' tools for measuring performance, and of course limitations in the way in which learning is designed and managed in the context of the business. At an individual level, even where careful consideration has been given to the construction of learning activities, the performance outcomes are not always as predicted or promised. Even where personal learning is achieved, there are many reasons why the wider workplace may not benefit, or indeed want to benefit. Where there are huge disparities in rewards and security, conditional access to positions of power, structural inequalities in the development of careers and inherently different perceptions of organisational goals and priorities, learning is bound to be hampered by careerism, anxiety, stress, deference and unresolved conflict. Even where such 'interference' to learning is minimal, mechanisms need to be in place which link individual to collective learning.

Chapter 7

National context and culture

Chapter overview

The relationship between workplace learning and performance improvement, as we observed in the last chapter, is relatively weak in the UK. Commentators ascribe this situation largely to prevailing institutional and cultural factors that do little to provide a supportive climate for workplace learning, and at worst place real constraints in the way of companies wishing to move more assertively in this direction (Finegold and Levine, 1997; Keep and Mayhew, 1996). Individual companies where workplace learning is well embedded are widely perceived as having succeeded 'against the odds' or by dint of strong local factors such as a committed managing director.

In some other countries, workplace learning is strongly supported by institutional arrangements and what might loosely be described as 'national culture'. These create a favourable and receptive climate for workplace learning, increasing the likelihood that learning will translate into positive performance outcomes. Japan, Germany and various of the 'tiger economies' are usually singled out as countries that have a strong workplace learning tradition, leading to a highly skilled workforce coupled with high productivity.

In this chapter, we look at the national context within which workplace learning takes place, drawing on examples from various countries to illustrate the complex interdependency between socio-economic, political and cultural variables which set the parameters for workplace learning at a national level and shape the nature and scope of workplace learning at the level of the individual firm. Productive organisations are never wholly conditioned by these national contexts, but neither are they entirely free from them.

Workplace learning arrangements, methodologies and practices are embedded in these institutional contexts, and their transfer across organisational and national boundaries depends among other things on the symmetry between the settings. Successful transferability calls for a sophisticated adaptation process.

The workplace in its institutional, social and cultural context

An understanding of the embeddedness of workplace learning in its institutional, social and cultural context is important when it comes to borrowing 'good practices' from one setting and transplanting them into another. Whether at the level of policy, methodology or technique, successful transfer is dependent on recognising that application and interpretation of a given concept are contextually dependent. As Turbin et al (1995) argues, concepts and practices are not easily transferred between cultures and contexts. Tools and simple techniques may be more easily transferred, while more complex practices cannot be transferred without specific understanding of context.

Different researchers have given different emphasis to institutional, societal and cultural factors when accounting for some of the major differences between countries in the approach taken to workplace learning. In the search for factors explaining Japan's competitive advantage, for example, there have been different but complementary lines of enquiry. Socio-cultural explanations for Japan's success predominated in an initial phase of the debate. Dore and Sako (1989) were among those identifying cultural factors (groupism, paternalism, lifelong employment, corporate welfarism, the competitive drive to improve life chances) as lying behind the distinctive approach to the use of human resources and lifetime learning. Since these features appeared to be specific to Japan (or Eastern cultures more generally), exporting the Japanese model of industrial production (with its integral system of on-the-job training) was not deemed feasible. In the second phase of the debate, emphasis shifted to institutional factors as these were played out at the level of the firm. The success of the Japanese companies was thought now to stem from just-in-time methodologies, stable and trusted networks of suppliers and managerial strategies, which could more readily be emulated by Western competitors. Koike and Inoke (1990), for example, argues that the process of lifetime learning which characterises Japanese manufacturing companies is explained by the way in which work is organised. What he sees as the 'integrated system' of organising the production process involves managers being systematically assessed in terms of their ability to transmit knowledge to their subordinates. In a third phase of the debate, Nonaka and Takeuchi (1995) return to the cultural specificity of Japan, but with a substantial difference with respect to the explanations advanced in the initial phase. The culture they draw on is not some anthropological 'substratum' of customs and beliefs, but rather the epistemological categories that underpin a vision of the world. And the roots of these categories Nonaka and Takeuchi discern in the different philosophical traditions of the two civilisations of East and West. The success of Japanese firms in an age when knowledge creation is seen as the key strategic resource is seen to reside in distinctive Eastern 'cognitive processes'.

Frade (1997) draws together the cultural and institutional aspects in the idea of 'learning patrimony'. This refers to the series of prevailing educational arrangements and practices, pedagogic dispositions, expectations and aspirations characteristic of a society or culture. Learning patrimony refers thus on the one hand to the way in which education and training are institutionalised through legislative, regulating frameworks and bodies, and on the other to the values, dispositions and attitudes with respect to education and training. These are in part manifested in broad educational philosophies about what education and training is for, as well as preferred learning styles and pedagogic practices. In Britain, for example, the liberal humanistic philosophy has been a significant influence on both institutional and learner behaviours, although muted in today's economic climate. In the Netherlands, in contrast, a more liberal or utilitarian view prevails, which manifests itself in a stress on practical knowledge and close links between companies and schools. Learning patrimony is not static or immutable – changes in the learning patrimony occur not only when the cultural context, in the broadest sense, demands such changes, but they can also be induced, if not directed, by the implementation of educational policies. The most powerful driver of educational change or reform is the economy.

Other researchers taking a societal approach to education and training systems in different national contexts have given primacy to social relations. Commonly associated with the work of Maurice (1994), the studies undertaken have been principally concerned with demonstrating differences between countries in relation to organisational configurations, work structuring and work co-ordination and the qualification and career systems. The social relations dimension is concerned with such aspects as relationships between employers and employees, attitudes to authority, conflict resolution and motivational structures, and the way union/management relations impact on the strategies of firms. While the societal school stresses cultural differences it does not treat culture as a separately defined variable but sees it embedded within the institutional arrangements as a whole. The main body of research has focused on France and Germany, and more recently Japan. The important point made by this research is that the work organisation in enterprises in the respective countries tends to legitimise and reinforce the way the education system is structured. You cannot, therefore, understand the development and operation of a national system of skill formation – including workplace learning within this – without simultaneously understanding the organisation of work within enterprises and the relationship between these two levels.

Cross-national differences

In the remaining part of this chapter we look at cross-national differences with respect to learning culture and context. In particular, we focus on those aspects that are relevant to the creation of a learning environment and performance improvement. These include the readiness or preparedness of workers for continuous training and learning in the workplace; the organisation and management of training in the workplace including employers' attitudes; and the regulatory policies and frameworks including the incentives for training.

Research evidence that exists on this broad topic of national culture and context can be mapped at three different levels:

- the level of the learner

- the level of employers or enterprises or other forms of organisation

- the more general infrastructure for the delivery of education and training and the values within society as a whole.

Our focus is primarily on the first two levels, with a brief consideration of the role of the state.

The learning patrimony that is characteristic of different countries is manifest in the educational profiles of those entering the workforce, in their preferences for certain kinds of work and in the attitudes towards continuing learning as an important activity throughout the adult life course. Cultural patterns of this kind impinge in significant ways on the readiness or preparedness of workers for learning in the workplace, including their capacity to be self-managing and self-directed.

The 'learner' level

A number of comparative studies have explored the 'learner-based' aspect of national learning culture, and in most countries there is also a strong research literature which informs national profiling of this kind. Germany and Japan figure strongly as comparators, usually taken as positive models in contrast to perceived shortcomings of the UK learning patrimony. Bynner and Roberts (1991), in their careful study of Anglo and German youth entering the workforce, are exceptional in drawing out the distinctive benefits of the two different systems for different sub-sectors of the youth population in differing economic circumstances. While patterns are clearly evident, education systems everywhere are changing and, among European countries at least, there are signs of convergence in response to globalising economic forces (Frade, 1997). For a rounded view of learner worker behaviours and attitudes in different national contexts it is also important, therefore, to look at recent research which may modify some of the more established conceptions about national differences.

The national learning culture in the UK displays these dual characteristics of constancy and change. Historically, the liberal–humanist tradition has been the underpinning educational philosophy with a corresponding antipathy to non-intellectual work – expressed in the continuing British angst about closer links between industry and the education system at whatever level. In recent years, a more utilitarian educational philosophy has gained hold, most evident in the competence framework of the national vocational qualifications which is strongest in the VET system but which increasingly encroaches on higher education as well. The lack of any mandatory requirement for continuing contact with education after age 16, coupled with weak routes back into education, has meant that a large proportion of the population hitherto has entered the workforce with a low level of skills and reduced opportunity for skill formation via the formal education system. UK students detach themselves from the education system earlier than their continental counterparts, and usually pursue a variety of routes towards an occupational goal – part of the British culture of 'individualism' and civil liberties. While studies have shown strong support among new workers for learning on the job and an expectation of acquiring skills in this way rather than through training (Bynner and Roberts, 1991), the jobs are characteristically low skill in a 'learning-poor' work setting. The prevailing view seems to be that whatever you need to know in a job can be taught on the job itself; getting the job is what matters. As these researchers note, 'training as preliminary to employment has not penetrated deeply into the British psyche'. Regulatory arrangements supportive of this low-skills approach are reflected in the very few occupations in Britain where VET must deliver prescribed learning experiences before individuals can practise.

New research on changing skills in Britain modifies this picture (Green et al, 1997). Their analysis of skill trends, comparing 1997 with 1996, indicates that participation rates in post-compulsory education have increased with a corresponding increase in the proportion of workers who possess a qualification. Furthermore, there has been an unambiguous increase in the qualification level that new recruits are now required to have. Whereas 62 per cent of jobs required at least some qualification in 1986, by 1997 this had risen to 69 per cent. For 'high level' qualifications (anything above A-level) the proportion rose from 20 per cent to 24 per cent. While a greater proportion of the workforce now has a degree or better so, too, a greater proportion of jobs are demanding degrees. The 1997 jobs are also less likely to require very short periods of training and less likely to need only a short time to acquire proficiency. At both ends of the occupational spectrum there is evidence of rising skills. All in all, the researchers are cautiously optimistic in seeing these changes as movement towards a 'learning society', if only piecemeal and partial.

In an earlier chapter we also cited research findings from a study conducted for the RSA by MORI, which showed that people have varying though generally positive attitudes towards learning, but that significant barriers such as lack of money and time stood in the way of their increasing participation in learning activities. Research undertaken as part of the ESRC Learning Society programme has shown how individual motivation is in part shaped by the structural opportunities and incentives that confront the individual.

While Britain may be closing the gap with its competitor nations in educational and skill levels, it is undoubtedly true that other countries have a longer tradition and firmer base on which to build the capabilities of their workforce for the new economy. In a comparative study of Britain and Canada, Ashton, Green and Lowe (1993) found significant differences between the two countries in the pattern of school-to-work transition, fostering in Canadian learner workers a greater acceptance of education as an important activity throughout the adult life course. There was more of a culture of individual responsibility for learning, reflected in the finding that, overall, twice as many people in Canada as in the UK were pursuing some form of education as part of ongoing learning at work.

In Germany, it is taken for granted that all young people must receive all-round preparation for entry to work and adulthood, and must be qualified to enter employment (Bynner and Roberts, 1991). The growth of participation in education and training has brought about a considerable improvement in the structure of qualifications and competence among the working population. Over 80 per cent of the German working population now hold vocational or professional qualifications, and by 2010 this percentage is expected to be 90 per cent of the working population.

The German learning patrimony, with its strong integration of vocational education and training, continues the tradition of mediaeval guild training, as practised all over Europe. However, in contrast to other countries, this system of practical and theoretical learning was adapted for the purposes of industry in the 19th and 20th centuries and was brought together into a modern vocational training system. The centrepiece of this is the dual system, which provides employer-provided training with part-time education at vocational schools. As a system, it thrives through progressive development in which employers, unions, government and research institutes share. West Germany has experienced ever rising educational achievement of school leavers in the past three decades, with many people using more than one opportunity during the upper secondary years to improve their competence. It is commonplace, for example, for individuals to complete two years full-time vocational schooling followed by training in the dual system. Today, about two-thirds of young people start their training in the dual system while just 15 years ago it was less than 50 per cent. A vocational qualification confers high standing, where it is recognised that a highly qualified workforce is necessary for Germany to succeed in international competition (Schmidt and Alex, 1995). Bynner and Roberts (1991) comment that the apprenticeship system is much more likely to have equipped young people with a set of 'enabling skills' (learning to learn, expectations that they will have to continue to learn, and so on). At the same time, however, they note that German-style apprentice training has never been a necessary condition for forming competitive industrial workforces. Sweden, the USA and Japan have been successful industrial economies without a dual system – each organises the transition into employment in its own distinctive way.

Japan has the highest education participation in the world, with more young people remaining in education for longer periods than their counterparts in other countries. Without doubt, employers are served with a steady supply of highly educated and particularly numerate labour recruits. In marked contrast with Germany, however, the Japanese have relatively little formal vocational education. General education, through academic routes, holds almost total sway within the education system, prior to people starting work. Within companies, work and learning are intertwined in programmes of systematic development which makes relatively little use of formal vocational education.

Japanese students tend to have broad-based knowledge, good self-discipline, self-reliant study capabilities and generally conformist attitudes (Oram, 1995). Two forces in Japanese school education – the competitive drive to improve life chances and the older Confucian traditions (the belief that self-development and self-cultivation are desirable in themselves and a condition for citizen self-respect) – make acceptable a high intensity of schooling (Dore and Sako, 1989).

Japan does not merely aim for increased education participation rates and higher standards. These are used to provide a dynamic foundation for continuous learning, based on a variety of delivery mechanisms. The most important condition for successful implementation of the skill formation system is a positive attitude to learning among those participating. The school provides a solid kick-start in developing the attitudes and practices that support self-directed learning, in producing people who are capable of following carefully detailed and complex written instructions that support learning on the job with the use of manuals and instructional materials, and in generally providing the basis for individual competence and a sense of self-efficacy.

A key feature of the Japanese learning patrimony identified by Dore and Sako (1989) is the kind of moral feelings that the Japanese have about needing to be good at their jobs. Historically, the Japanese education system was built alongside, and in support of, the formation of the modern industrial society and nation state, to train each citizen uniformly to be a dedicated worker. There is a strong emphasis on national interest and efficiency, rather than on individual self-fulfilment.

In recent years there has been some questioning of the continuing appropriateness of Japanese cultural values and their reflection in educational practices. The modern workplace socio-economic restructuring is disturbing the established patterns and consonance. Not only is the old industrial framework that worked well for Japan's manufacturing industries under challenge from the new network system of the information-based economy, but the relevance of the education system which historically closely paralleled the manufacturing system is being seriously questioned (Sawano, 1997). Whereas emphasis in the past was on equality and uniformity, increased emphasis in schools is to be placed in future on developing more diverse competences, including creativity and critical thinking. In comparison with British students at the upper capability levels, Japanese school leavers and those graduating from college and university are seen as having very good knowledge but less analytical skill in applying it. Social skills are limited, and do not include debating, questioning and challenging skills (Oram, 1995). Whereas bright and malleable students were suited to a manufacturing system overlaid on Taylorism and Fordism, the emphasis on continuous improvement in today's company requires a capability for knowledge creation, flexibility and the tapping of tacit and often highly subjective insights, intuitions and hunches (Nonaka, 1996). The school system is seen as having a key role to play in developing the 'learning to learn' skills of future workers and fostering a readiness in employees to question existing premisses and make sense of their experience in a new way.

Employers and enterprise level

The work of researchers such as Marsden, Streeck and Koike and Inoike have been important in demonstrating the links between the organisation of work and the organisation of training, explored in different national contexts. In parallel with, and complementary to, this work has been the contribution of the societal approach, associated with researchers working at Laboratoire d'Economie et de Sociologie du Travail in France (Maurice, Sorge and Warner).

The main body of research has been concerned with France, Germany and Japan. The relative paucity of material on the UK reflects the relatively weak support systems in place for systematised workplace learning, and what Mayhew and Keep (1996) refer to as the problem of 'managerial failure' which they consider to be particularly prevalent in Britain. The strong preference for a low-skilled route, relying on cost-competitiveness, not only limits the demand for skilled labour but means that employers have relatively little incentive to put into effect the range of organisational measures that would support effective workplace learning. Mayhew and Keep advance a number of reasons for this situation. First, that managers have been brought up in a confrontational system of industrial relations where workers are not required to think, and where initiative and talent are required of only a minority. Second, that training is a positional good, more of which may threaten existing power relationships. Third, the volatility of the British economy makes returns to training harder to quantify than easily comprehended costs. And fourth, that short-termism has become institutionalised in Britain through a variety of mechanisms.

France, Germany and Japan, in contrast to the UK, have strong support structures for in-company skill formation, and established linkages between educational provision and work organisation. There are, nonetheless, significant differences between these three countries, as summarised in Figure 6 overleaf.

Two features of the German skill formation system at enterprise level are worth highlighting. First, there is a strong social partnership between the government, trade unions and employers at the core of vocational training. The system displays a highly corporatist structure, with employers, employees and the state monitoring the quality of vocational training in the framework of a highly institutionalised system of consultation. The discussion about on-the job learning in the course of a career is also characterised by an emphasis on institutionalising and formalising learning processes (Onstenk, 1995b). It is noteworthy that this highly regulated initial vocational training system is complemented, however, by a largely unregulated continuing training system, in which the focus of what regulation there is is not the company but protection of the consumer of training services (Drake, 1995).

The second key feature of the German system is the vital role played by the Meister, both in direct support of training and in the development of a training culture (Brown et al, 1994). The German Meister system is part and parcel of a culture

Figure 6   Key findings - France, Germany and Japan

Country	Educational provision	Work organisation	Linkages
France	• hierarchiacally organised model • superiority of academic over vocational	• internal hierarchies stress seniority and internal promotion • administrative means of managing human resources	• employers are distanced from vocational training • qualifications do not correspond to type of job • employers' human resource strategies devalue vocational education
Germany	• vocational and general training are complementary • dual system for post-compulsory education	• work organisation is structured around training system (eg role of Meister and trainee status) • autonomy of supervisors and responsibility of skilled workers	• dual system mostly managed by employers who fund two-thirds • occupational markets ensure the value of vocational education and training
Japan	• school-based model for initial vocational preparation with strong bias towards general education • superiority of academic over vocational • companies responsible for vocational training	• work organisation characterised by internal markets and mobility • on-the-job training with mentorship system, collective learning • implicit contracts between employers and employees	• no apparent links between general education and in-company training and vocational education in schools is not emphasised • specific recruitment links between schools and enterprises

Source: Adaped from Maurice (1992,1993,1994)

and structure which offers strong incentives, in the forms of pay and status. The pay differential encourages Meisters to follow training in their own time, and the qualification itself is highly marketable because of the broad competencies involved and its established status.

Brown et al (1994) note in their comparative study of key workers the whole framework of support that accounts for the effectiveness of the German Meister and the difficulty of transposing this model into other national contexts:

> The strategic importance of the Meister can hardly be overstated. Over a quarter of those completing apprenticeships go eventually to attain Meister status. Hence Meister are realistic role models. The Meister training combines organisational, supervisory and technical training with explicit training in pedagogics. The vocational route, and vocational qualifications, are highly respected with clear opportunities for career advancement in many industries. So once again, progression within industry as a whole is tied to personal learning development, one important element of which is the ability to facilitate learning in others.

Those undertaking Meister training have also to be able to develop training competence in others, hence more 'key workers' (with or without full Meister qualifications) are embedded in the structure of work. The experienced Meister, with heavy organisational responsibilities, may spend comparatively little time engaged in direct informal support. However, the training culture is such that workers, working alongside or close to others, are expected to assist the development of other workers, and to demonstrate that they have the key skills of facilitating and supporting learning.

In sum, there are three key features of the environment and infrastructure that support the German model of skill development in a company setting. First, a mechanism that allows a prospective Meister to develop the skills of guidance, facilitation and support. Second, a training culture that allows the coach to exemplify a continuing commitment to learning. And third, a framework for career advancement and progression that supports the continuing development of expertise as a coach.

Japan also has a highly developed system of company-based skills formation, supported by a raft of organisational policies. As in Germany, the role, training and attitude of managers and supervisors is of considerable importance. Training of trainers is both implicit and explicit. So is the time that managers and supervisors contribute to training, estimated at more than 20 per cent. It is widely considered that the most important managerial responsibility in Japan is the development of staff (Oram, 1995).

On-the-job training in Japan is best described as a methodology rather than a method. It comprises a progressive cycle: it is not *ad hoc* and is planned and prepared for. Moreover, such methodologies are consistently applied over a much wider span of occupations than the 'shop floor'.

Among the important internal organisational factors which support Japanese in-company learning, as identified in the work of Koike and Inoke (1990) and Dore and Sako (1989), are the following:

- wage payments which are designed to encourage long-term employment in order that complex skills can be mastered

- the linkage of award systems to general educational levels rather than to discrete occupational qualifications

- recruitment and selection criteria which concentrate first on demonstrated ability to learn rather than on particular job competences already acquired, and second on recruitment for a career, not a job.

HRD strategies which support

- the development of career paths within a specific enterprise

- reward systems which offer compensation through both salary and promotion for those who have made the effort

- a merit rating system that recognises and gives high preference to those who can handle unusual operations

- promotion systems whereby positions of foreman and supervisor are normally filled by production workers, and

- a general expectation that training is part of the supervisor's job – how well s/he bring on his or her junior workers is one of the criteria by which a senior worker will be rated.

Most Japanese employers accept that responsibility for training is theirs. They are sensitive, however, to the kind of learning they can be expected to pay for and what the state and individuals should support. Expenditure by Japan on training is not high in comparison with other countries. Where Japan does compare well is in the value it gets from synergistic integration of appropriate initiatives.

The institutional level

In the UK, the government has relied on the market to determine both the direction in which the economy moves and also, in recent years, the delivery of training. The state merely guarantees the legal framework. The limitations of a market-led system of training have been well documented (Booth and Snower, 1996; Keep and Mayhew, 1996; Finegold and Levine, 1997). France, Australia and Sweden (as well as Japan and Germany) are among those countries whose training policies reflect a view that market incentives are grossly insufficient to generate the socially desirable amount of investment in skills. Measures include systems of training levies, retraining support for the unemployed, institutional bonds between employers and employees, to name a few. Canada and the Netherlands have recently identified enabling measures required of government to support a strong continuing training and learning workforce.

Recent research on the political economy of skill formation in East Asian newly industrialised economies explores a different model, linking skill formation with the role of the state in economic development. The new model demonstrates how the agencies of state can develop the skills of the labour force, not just through enhancing educational provision for those entering the labour market but by acting directly on employers and individuals in the workplace. The basis for assessing skill needs is not the individual employer, as in the West or Japan, but the government's future economic goals. The success of the 'tiger economies' stems from their ability to link skill formation policy closely to specific stages of economic development. Training policy is then directed at ensuring that the human resources are in place to provide the level of skill formation necessary to attract the relevant industries and ensure that they are competitive in world markets.

Ashton and Turbin (1995) have documented both the cultural borrowing by the Singaporeans from the German dual system, the Japanese on-the-job training and the UK open learning experience, and the difficulties subsequently experienced in transposing these into their national context. Particular examples of barriers were the differences in labour market structure and work opportunities between Germany, Japan and Singapore. This was reflected in the training practices of employers, the shortage of qualified trainers and supervisors and the hostility towards passing on skills to subordinates. It may also be, they suggest, that cultural values such as the values placed upon training and learning, may also act as barriers. The stronger hierarchical organisation of work, for example, may make it more difficult to move towards a more open structure where supervisors feel able to pass on skills without feeling their own job or position is at risk.

The transfer of learning methods, arrangements and practices into new contexts

Culture, in both its organisational and national sense, is an important factor that can facilitate or impede the effective transfer of learning methods and arrangements from one context, organisation or country to another. Although there is disagreement as to which of these cultures is more important, with Hofstede (1994b) insisting that national culture is more important than organisational culture and Kanter (1995) arguing the opposite, there is little doubt that culture and the various sub-cultures influence international, inter-sectoral, inter-organisational, and even intra-organisational co-operation and transfer. This clearly has a number of implications for the transfer potential of workplace learning innovations between companies, sectors and nations, with research highlighting also the importance of cultural fit or symmetry between the actors involved in transfer.

Whether or not a learning method(ology) can be successfully transferred across contexts is dependent on the 'object' of transfer and how 'tangible' (and therefore contextualised) it is, as well as on the degree of fit between settings of the perceived barriers to transfer. Transfer of knowledge and know-how or transfer of products between similar settings requires no adaptation, while transfer of training products or methods between dissimilar settings requires a sophisticated adaptation process. In general, the higher the level of contextualisation of the object of transfer, eg training methodologies, firm-specific training, management of training resources, the more difficult the transferability. Alternatively, the lower the level of contextualisation, eg generic training materials, principles of training or delivery systems, the easier the process of transfer.

Research has identified a plethora of factors that can impede the transfer process. These include differences in the orientation of national policy and/or company strategy; incompatibility of culture between host and receiving country; differences in the organisation and regulation of education and training; attitudes to VET in different settings and between different groups; differences in the values placed upon training by groups within or between societies; differences and rigidities in institutional arrangements; stage of industrial development, etc.

At the same time, research has highlighted conditions/factors that can 'facilitate' transfer. These include organisational, structural and strategic symmetry. Overall, there is a positive relationship between transferability and homogeneity, longevity, similarity in goals and complementarity in market position.

It makes most sense to approach 'transfer' of training and learning methods, arrangements and practices as a process rather than a mechanical 'move' of some tangible object. One needs, therefore, to understand the context within which the 'model' or training solution has emerged, the context, needs and capacity of the receiving organisation, and the actual process of adoption, including adaptation and embedding.

References and further reading

Adler, P. and R. Cole (1993) 'Designed for learning: a tale of two auto plants', *Sloan Management Review* Spring: 85-94.

Andrews, F. (1979) Scientific Productivity. *The Effectiveness of Research Groups in Six Countries*. Cambridge: Cambridge University Press.

ARTICULATE (1995) Evaluation of the DELTA Pilot Projects in the EU DELTA Programme. London: Tavistock Institute.

Ashton, D., F. Green and G. Lowe (1993) 'The linkages between education and employment: a comparative study of Britain and Canada', *Comparative Education* 29(2): 125-43.

Ashton, D. and J. Turbin (1995). *Research Action on Transferability of Training and Learning :case study on cross-national transferability*. London: Tavistock Institute.

Ashton, D., M. Maguire and M. Spilsbury (1990) *Restructuring the Labour Market: Implications for youth*. London: Macmillan.

Baxi Heating (1993) 'Employee development in Baxi Heating' in K. Forrester, J. Payne and K. Ward, eds *Developing a Learning Workforce*. Leeds: University of Leeds.

Becker, B. and M. Huselid, (1998) 'High performance work systems and firm performance: a synthesis of research and managerial implications', *Research in Personnel and Human Resource Management*, Vol 16.

Bengtsson, J. (1993) 'Labour markets of the future: the challenge to the education policy markers', *European Journal of Education* 28(2): 135-57.

Bennett, R., H. Glennerster and D. Nevison (1992) *Learning should Pay*. Poole: British Petroleum

Betcherman, G., K. McMullen and K. Davidman (1998) *Training for the New Economy*. Ottawa: Canadian Policy Research Networks Inc.

Black, S. and L. Lynch (1997) *How to Compete: The impact of workplace practices and information*. NBER Working Paper No. 6120.

Blundell, R., L. Dearden and M. Costas (1995) *The Determinants and Effects of Training in Britain: Final report*. London: Institute for Fiscal Studies, University College London.

Booth, A. and D. Snower (eds) (1996) *Acquiring Skills. Market failures, their symptoms and policy responses*. Cambridge: Cambridge University Press.

Bosworth, D., C. Jacobs and J. Lewis (1990) *New Technologies, Shared Facilities and the Innovatory Firm*. Aldershot: Avebury.

Brown, A., K. Evans, S. Blackman and S. Germon (1994) *Key Workers: Technical and Training Mastery in the Workplace*. Bournemouth: Hyde.

Brown J. and P. Duguid (1991) 'Organisational learning and communities of practice: toward a unified view of working, learning and innovation', *Organisation Science* 2(1): 40-57.

Brown P. and R. Scase (1991) eds *Poor Work: Disadvantage and the division of labour*. Milton Keynes: Open University Press.

Brown, A. (1994) 'Recent developments in the clothing industry' in A. Brown, K. Evans, S. Blackman and S. Germon (1994) *Key Workers: technical and training mastery in the workplace*. Bournemouth: Hyde.

Bunk, G. (1994) 'Teaching competence in initial and continuing vocational training in the Federal Republic of Germany', *European Journal of Vocational Training* 1: 8–14.

Bynner, J. and K. Roberts (1991) *Youth and Work: Transition to employment in England and Germany*. London: Anglo-German Foundation.

Candy. P. and J. Matthews (1998) 'Fusing learning and work: changing conceptions of workplace learning' in D. Boud (ed.) *Workplace Learning: Current research and new agendas*. Adelaide: National Centre for Vocational Education Research.

Cassels, J. (1990) *Britain's Real Skill Shortage*. London: Policy Studies Institute.

CBI (1991) *Competing with the World's Best – The report of the CBI Manufacturing Advisory Group*. London: Confederation of British Industry.

CBI (1992) *Focus on the First Line: The role of the supervisor*. London: Confederation of British Industry.

CBI (1994) *Flexible Labour Markets*. London:Confederation of British Industry.

Coopers and Lybrand Associates (1985) *A Challenge to Complacency: Changing attitudes to training*. Sheffield: Manpower Services Commission.

Coopey, J. (1996) 'Crucial gaps in "the learning organisation": power, politics and ideology', in K. Starkey (ed.) *How Organisations Learn*. London: International Thomson Publishing.

Cullen, J. (1998) 'Promoting competitiveness for small business clusters through collaborative learning' in M. Steiner (ed.). *Clusters and Regional Specialisation*, London: Prion.

Cullen, J. and E. Sommerlad (1997) 'Making sense of organisational learning in small to medium enterprises', *Tavistock Review*. London: Tavistock Institute.

Danau, D. and E. Sommerlad (1996) *Workplace Learning*. Maastricht: European Centre for Work and Society.

Dankbaar, B. (1995) 'Learning to meet the global challenge: a contribution to the debate on continuing vocational training in the automotive industry of the CVT/FORCE' Automobile Network: MERIT.

Darrah, C. (1995) 'Workplace training, workplace learning: a case study', *Human Organization* 54(1): 31-41.

Dawson, P. and J. Webb (1989) 'New production arrangements: the totally flexible cage', *Work, Employment and Society* 3(2).

Dehnbostel, P. (1996) Increasing the attractiveness of vocational training for young people. Unpublished manuscript. Berlin: BIBB.

Dench, S. (1993) Working Papers 3, 4 and 5. *Employment Department Social Science Research Branch*.

Dixon, N. (1994) *The Organisational Learning Cycle. How we can learn collectively*. New York: McGraw Hill.

Docherty, P. (1994) *Learning at Work*. Stockholm: Swedish Work Environment Fund.

Dore. R. and M. Sako (1989) *How the Japanese Love to Work*. London: Routledge.

Drake, K. (1995) 'The economics of learning on-the-job. A European perspective on instruction-led and experience-led job competence.' Paper for conference on Efficiency and Equity in Education Policy, Canberra, 1995.

Dyson, K. (1990) *Small and Medium Enterprise*. London: Routledge.

Engerstrom, Y. (1994) *Training for Change. A new approach to instruction and learning in training*. ILO: Geneva.

Eraut, M., J. Alderton, G. Cole and P. Senker (1998) Development of Knowledge and Skills in Employment. Final Report on a Research Project funded by 'The Learning Society' Programme of the Economic and Social Research Council, UK.

European Centre for Work and Society in co-operation with the Tavistock Institute (1996) Work Based Learning Report to DGXXII, European Commission.

EUROTECNET (1993) *Key/Core Competences: Synthesis of work in Eurotecnet programme*. Brussels: European Commission.

Evans, K., A. Brown and T. Oates (1987) *Developing Work-based Learning*. Sheffield: Employment Department.

Feerman, L. , M. Hoyman, J. Cutcher-Gershenfeld and E. Savoie (eds) (1991). *Joint Training Programmes: A union-management approach to preparing workers for the future*. New York: Cornell University.

FEFC (1994) *Education and Employments in the Further Education Sector in England*. Coventry: Further Education Funding Council.

Felstead, A. and F. Green (1996) 'Training implications of regulation compliance and business cycles' in A. Booth and D. Snower, (eds.) *Acquiring Skills*. Cambridge: Cambridge University Press.

Felstead, A., D. Ashton, F. Green and J. Sung (1994) *International Study of Vocational Education and Training in the Republic of Germany, France, Japan, Singapore and the United States*. Leicester: Centre for Labour Market Studies, University of Leicester.

Finegold, D. (1991) 'Institutional incentives and skill creation: preconditions for a high-skill equilibrium' in P. Ryan (ed.) *International Comparisons of Vocational Education and Training for Intermediate Skills*, London: Falmer.

Finegold, D. and D. Levine (1997) 'Institutional incentives for employer training', *Journal of Education and Work* 10(2): 109-27.

Finegold, D. and D. Soskice (1988) 'The failure of training in Britain: analysis and prescription', *Oxford Review of Economic Policy* 2(2): 21-53.

Forrester, K., J. Payne and K. Ward, (eds) (1993) *Developing a Learning Workforce*. Leeds: University of Leeds.

Forrester, K., J. Payne and K. Ward (1995a) 'Lifelong education and the workplace: a critical analysis', *International Journal of Lifelong Education* 14(4): 292-305.

Forrester, K., J. Payne and K. Ward (1995b) *Workplace Learning: Perspectives on Education, Training and Work*. Aldershot: Avebury.

Frade, C. (1995) 'Models and theories of learning' in D. Danau and E. Sommerlad (eds) *Work Based Learning*. Maastrict: European Centre for Work and Society.

Frade, C. (1997) Socio-cultural, economic and policy aspects of education and learning innovations. TSER Delilah Consortium. Deliverable 01. London: Tavistock Institute.

Fryer, R. (1997) *Learning for the Twenty-First Century*. First Report of the National Advisory Group for Continuing Education and Lifelong Learning. (No publication details given)

Gallie, D. and M. White (1993) *Employee Commitment and the Skills Revolution*. London: Policy Studies Institute.

Grant, R., R. Shani, and R. Krishnan (1994), 'TQM's challenge to management theory and practice' *Sloan Management Review*, Winter: 29-33.

Green, F., D. Ashton, B. Burchell, B. Davies and A. Felstead (1997) 'An analysis of changing work skills in Britain'. Paper presented to the Low Wage Employment Conference of the European Low-Wage Employment Research Network, Centre for Economic Performance, London School of Economics.

Greenhalgh, C. and G. Mavrotas (1993) 'Workforce training in the Thatcher era – Market Forces and Market Failures', *International Journal of Manpower* 14(2): 17-32.

Hakim, C. (1989) 'New recruits to self-employment in the 1980s', *Employment Gazette*, June: 286-97.

Hart, M. (1993) 'Educative or miseducative work: a critique of the current debate on work and education', *Canadian Journal of Adult Education* May: 21-36.

Hatton, M., (ed) (1996) *Lifelong Learning. Policies, Practices and Programs*. Ontario: School of Media Studies, Toronto: Humber College.

Hendricks, K. and V. Singhal (1994) *Quality Awards and the Market Value of the Firm*. Working Paper, College of William and Mary.

Hendry, C., A. Jones and A. Pettigrew (1991) *Human Resource Development in Small to Medium Enterprises*. Research Paper 88. Sheffield: Employment Department.

Hillage, J. and J. Moralee (1996) *The Return on Investors*. Brighton: The Institute for Employment Studies.

Hines T. and R. Thorpe (1995) 'New approaches to understanding small firm networks – the key to performance managerial learning and development'. Paper presented at the ISBA National Conference, Paisley, 1995.

Hofstede, G. (1994a) 'Management scientists are human', *Management Science* 40(1):4-13.

Hofstede, G. (1994b) *Culture and Organisations*. Software of the Mind, London: HarperCollins.

Hugentobler, M. and R. Keller, (1993) 'Workplace learning and redesign initiatives in Switzerland' in K. Forrester, J. Payne and K. Ward (eds) *Developing a Learning Workforce*. Leeds: University of Leeds.

Hyland,T. and H. Matlay (1997) 'Small businesses, training needs and VET provision', *Journal of Education and Work* 10 (2): 129-39.

Hyman, J. (1992) *Training at Work: A critical analysis of policy and practice*. London: Routledge.

Ichiniowski, C., T. Kochan, D. Levine, C. Olson and G. Strauss (1996) 'What works at work' *Industrial Relations* 35(3): 249-333.

Ichiniowski, C., K. Shaw and G. Prennushi (1994) The effects of human resource management practices on productivity. Unpublished manuscript.

IES (1995) *Employers' Use of the NVQ System*. University of Sussex: Institute of Employment Studies.

ILO (1998) World Employment Report 1998–99: employability in the global economy – how training matters. Geneva: International Labour Office.

Industrial Society (various years) *The Industrial Society's Training Trends Surveys*. London: Industrial Society.

James, G. (1991) *Quality of Working Life and Total Quality Management*. Work and Research Unit Occasional Paper No.50. London: ACAS/WRU

Jarrell, S. and Easton, G. (1994) 'An exploratory empirical investigation of the effects of total quality management on corporate performance' in P. Lederer (ed.) *The Practice of Quality Management*. Boston, Mass: Harvard Business School Press.

Jones, A. and C. Hendry (1994) 'The learning organisation: adult learning and organisational transformation', *British Journal of Management* 5: 153-62.

Kanter, R. M. (1995) *World Class: Thinking locally in the global economy*. New York: Simon and Schuster.

Katzenbach, J.R. and D.K Smith (1993) *The Wisdom of Teams: Creating the high performance organisation*. Boston, Mass. Havard Business School Press.

Keenoy, T. (1990) 'Human Resource Management: Rhetoric, Reality and Contradiction', *International Journal of Human Resource Management* 1(3) 363-84.

Keep, E. (1997) "There's no such thing as society ..." some problems with an individual approach to creating a learning society', *Journal of Education Policy* 12(6): 457-71.

Keep, E. and K. Mayhew (1994) *Scoping Paper for the 'What makes training pay' project*, London: Institute of Personnel and Development.

Keep, E. and K. Mayhew (1996) 'Evaluating the assumptions that underlie training policy' in A. Booth and D. Snower, (eds.) *Acquiring Skills. Market failures, their symptoms and policy responses*. Cambridge: Cambridge University Press.

Keep, E. and K. Mayhew (1997) 'Vocational education and training and economic performance' in T. Buxton, P. Chapman and P. Temple (eds), *Britain's Economic Performance* 2nd edn. London: Routledge.

Koike, K. and T. Inoke (1990) *Skill Formation in Japan and Southeast Asia*. Tokyo: University of Tokyo Press.

Kruijd, D. (ed) (1991) Opleiden op de werkple. [*Training in the workplace: handbook of training in organisations*] Deventer: Kluwer.

Lave, J. and E. Wenger (1991) *Situated learning: Legitimate peripheral participation*. Cambridge: Cambridge University Press.

Lawler, E. (1986) *High Involvement Management*. San Francisco: Jossey Bass.

Legge, K. (1995) *Human Resource Management: Rhetoric and Realities*. London: Macmillan Press.

Levy, M. (1991) *Work-based Learning: A good practice model*. Bristol: Further Education Staff College.

Levy, M. (1992) *Work-based Learning. Strategies for structuring learning opportunities in the workplace*. Bristol: Further Education Staff College.

Leys, M., Wigaerts D. and C. Hancke (1992) in A. Hendrikse 'Leittext' in D. Danau and E. Sommerlad (1995) *Work Based Learning*. Maastricht: European Centre for Work and Society.

Lloyd, C. and M. Rawlinson (1992) 'New technology and Human Resource Management', in P. Blyton and P. Turnbull (eds). *Reassessing Human Resource Management*. London: Sage.

Lynch, L. and S. Black (1995) *Beyond the Incidence of Training Evidence from a National Employers Program*. NBER Working Paper No 5231.

Marsick, V. (ed) (1987) *Learning in the Workplace*. London: Croom Helm.

Mason, G., B. Van Ark and K. Wagner (1994) 'Productivity, product quality and workforce skills: food processing in four European countries', *National Institute of Economic Review*. February.

Mason, G., B. Van Ark and K. Wagner (1996) 'Workforce skills, product quality and economic performance' in A. Booth and D. Snower, (eds) *Acquiring Skills. Market Failures, Their Symptons and Policy Responses*. Cambridge: Cambridge University Press.

Matlay, H. (1994) 'Training in the small business sector'. Paper presented at CERC Research Seminar. Department of Continuing Education: University of Warwick.

Matlay, H. (1996) 'Paradox resolved? Owner/manager attitudes to, and actual provision of, training in the small business sector of the British economy'. Paper presented at ISBA Conference, November, University of Birmingham.

Maurice, M. (1992) 'L'arrimage entre l'entreprise et le système d'éducation en matière formation professionnelle: le cas de France, de l'Allemagne et du Japon.' Paper presented to International Conference, University of Laval, Quebec.

Maurice, M. (1993) 'La formation professionnelle en France, en Allemagne et au Japon: trois types de relations entre l'école et l'entreprise.' *Entreprises et Histoire*, No.3.

Maurice, M. (1994) 'L'analyse sociétale des relations entre système éducatif et système productif: comparaisons France, Allemagne, Japon.' *Education et Pedagogies*.

Mayhew, K. and E. Keep (1996) 'Evaluating the assumptions that underlie training policy' in A. Booth and D. Snower, (eds.) *Acquiring Skills. Market Failures, their symptoms and policy responses*. Cambridge: Cambridge University Press.

McGill, I. and L. Beaty (1992) *Action Learning. A Practitioner's Guide*. London: Kogan Page.

McIlroy, J. (1997) Book Review of Workplace Learning (in K. Forrester et al. 1995b) *International Journal of Lifelong Education* 16(2): 156-69.

Mehaut, P. and J. Delcourt (1994) *The Role of the Enterprise in Generating Qualifications: The Training Impact of Work Organisation*. Synthesis of National Reports. Berlin: European Centre for the Development of Vocational Training (CEDEFOP).

Munnelly, C. (1987) 'Learning participation: The worker's viewpoint' in V. Marsick, (ed) *Learning in the Workplace*. London: Croom Helm.

Neumann, J., R. Holti and H. Standing (1995) *Change Everything at Once. Guide to Developing Teamwork in Manufacturing*. London: Management Books 2000 Ltd.

Nonaka, I. (1996) 'The knowledge-creating company', in K. Starkey (ed.) *How Organisations Learn*. London: International Thomson Publishing.

Nonaka, I. and H. Takeuchi (1995) *The Knowledge-creating Company*. Oxford: Oxford University Press.

Office of Science and Technology (1995) *Technology Foresight: Progress through partnership* – 2: Construction. London: HMSO.

Oliver, N. and B. Wilkinson (1988) *The Japanisation of British Industry*. Oxford. Blackwell.

Onstenk, J. (1992) Designing training programs for poorly educated employees. Unpublished manuscript.

Onstenk, J. (1993) On the job learning and on the job training. A survey of policies in six countries. Draft manuscript.

Onstenk, J. (1995a) 'Human resources development and on-the-job learning' in Mulder, M., W. Nijhof and R. Brinkerehoff (eds) *Corporate Training for Effective Performance*, Norwell: Kluwer Academic Publishers.

Onstenk, J. (1995b) Skill formation, on-the-job learning and on-the-job training. Introductory paper. Draft manuscript.

Onstenk, J. (1997a) 'First Dutch Interim Report to European Observatory on Innovation in Vocational Training.'

Onstenk, J. (1997b) Innovation, work teams and learning on-the-job. Paper for the EU Seminar on Knowledge and Work, Amsterdam.

Oram, M. (1995) 'Japanese in-company learning' NCE Briefing New Series 4. London: National Commission on Education.

Patterson, G.M., M.A. West, R. Lawthom and S. Nickell (1997) *The Impact of People Management Practices on Business Performance*. London: Institute of Personnel and Development.

Patriotta, G. and E. Sommerlad (1995) Bottlenecks and breakdowns: capturing the learning dynamics of the assembly line. Conference Proceedings of the ECLO Conference , Warwick University.

Pedler, M., J. Burgoyne and T. Boydell (1991) *The Learning Company: A Strategy for Sustainable Development*. Maidenhead: McGraw-Hill.

Rainbird, H. (1990) *Training Matters: Union Perspectives on Industrial Restructuring and Training*. Oxford: Blackwell.

Rainbird, H. (1994) 'Continuing training' in K. Sisson (ed.) *Personnel Management – A Comprehensive Guide to Theory and Practice in Britain*. Oxford: Blackwell.

Raizen, S. (1994) 'Learning and work: the research base', in *Vocational Education and Training for Youth: Towards Coherent Policy and Practice*, Paris: OECD.

Raper, P., D. Ashton, D. A. Felstead and J. Storey (1997) 'Towards the learning organisation: explaining current trends in training practice in the UK', *International Journal of Training and Development* 1(1).

Ravid, G. (1987) 'Self-directed learning in industry' in V. Marsick (ed.) *Learning in the Workplace*. London: Croom Helm.

Rosengarten, P. (1995) Learning organisations and their characteristics: the case of automotive components suppliers in Britain. Unpublished manuscript.

Royal Academy of Engineering (1996) *A statement on the Construction Industry*. London: Royal Academy of Engineering.

Russell, R. (1994) 'Mentoring at Marconi Underwater Systems Ltd: a case study' in Brown, A., K. Evans, S. Blackman and S. Germon *Key Workers: Technical and Training Mastery in the Workplace*. Bournemouth: Hyde.

Saggers, R.(1994) 'Training climbs the corporate agenda', *Personnel Management* July, 40-45.

Sargent, N., J. Field, H. Francis, T. Schuller and A. Tuckett (1997) cited in R. Fryer *Learning for the Twenty-First Century*. First Report of the National Advisory Group for Continuing Education and Lifelong Learning. (No publication details)

Sawano, Y.(1997) 'Lifelong learning: an instrument for improving school education in Japan', in M. Hatton (ed) *Lifelong Learning: Policies practices and programs*. Toronto: Humber College.

Schmidt, H. and Alex, L. (1995) 'The dual system of vocational education and training in Germany', *INCE Briefing New Series 3*. London: National Commission on Education.

Schmidt-Hackenberg, B. (1992) 'New methodologies for in-company vocational training and education: empirical case studies' in T. Plomp, J. Pieters and A. Feteris (eds) *European Conference on Educational Research*, Enschede, University of Twente.

Schon, D. (1983) *The Reflective Practitioner: How Professionals Think in Action*. London: Temple Smith.

Schuck, G. (1996) 'Intelligent technology, intelligent workers: A new pedagogy for the high-tech workplace', in K. Starkey (ed.) *How Organisations Learn*. London: International Thomson Publishing.

Scott, P. and A.Cockrill (1997) *Skills and Training in the Construction Industry: The UK Experience*. ESRC Learning Society Initiative: Project Working Paper. Cardiff: CASS/School of Education, University of Wales, Cardiff.

Sewell, G. and B. Wilkinson (1992) 'Someone to watch over me: surveillance, discipline and the Just-in-Time labour process', Sociology 26(2).

Shackleton, J. with L. Clarke, T. Lange and S. Walsh (1995) *Training for Employment in Western Europe and the United States*. Aldershot: Edward Elgar.

Sisson, K. and J. Storey (1993) *Managing Human Resources and Industrial Relations*. Milton Keynes: Open University Press.

Skruber, R. (1987) 'Organisations as clarifying learning environments' in V. Marsick, (ed.) *Learning in the Workplace*. London: Croom Helm.

Sommerlad, E. (1996) 'Case Study of Rover Learning Business' in D. Danau and E. Sommerlad, *Work Based Learning*, Maastricht: European Centre for Work and Society.

Starkey, K. (ed) (1996) *How Organisations Learn*. London: International Thomson Publishing.

Steedman, H. and K. Wagner (1989) 'Productivity, machinery and skills: clothing manufacture in Britain and Germany', *National Institute Economic Review* May, 40-57.

Tavistock Institute (1994) *Learning Theory and Learning Technology*. London: Tavistock Institute.

Tavistock Institute (1998a) Draft report on 'CVT: A comparative perspective' project funded under the Learning Society Programme, UK Economic and Social Research Council.

Tavistock Institute (1998b) Intermediate Report to EU DGXIII on European Observatory on Innovations in Vocational Training.

Tavistock Institute/Frade et al (1996) *Case Studies on Learning Configurations. An Appraisal of the Education and Training Services Piloted in the EU's DELTA Programme on Telematics for Distance and Flexible Learning*. Deliverable 15. London: Tavistock Institute.

Toronto, R. (1993) 'The UAW-Ford Life/Education Planning Program' in K. Forrester, J. Payne and K. Ward (eds) *Developing a Learning Workforce*. Leeds: University of Leeds.

Tuckman, A. (1994), 'The yellow brick road: TQM and the restructuring of organisation culture', *Organisation Studies* 15(5).

Turbin, J, D. Danau, I. Darmon, C. Frade and A. Hendrikse (1995) *Transferability of Training and Learning. Final Report*. Report prepared for the European Commission. London: Tavistock Institute.

Walsh, K., A. Green and H. Steedman (1993) 'The role of the company in generating skills. The learning effects of work organisation – United Kingdom', CEDEFOP Report. Thessaloniki: CEDEFOP.

Watkins, K. and V. Marsick (1993) *Sculpting the Learning Organisation*. San Francisco: Jossey Bass.

Watson, D. and R. Taylor (1998) *Lifelong Learning and the University. A Post-Dearing Agenda*. London: Falmer Press.

Weick, K. (1990) 'Technology as equivoque: sensemaking in new technologies', in P. Goodman and L. Sproull (eds) *Technology and Organisations*. San Francisco: Jossey Bass.

Weinstein, K. (1995) *Action Learning: A Journey in Discovery and Development*. London: Harper Collins.

Weiss, A. (1994) 'Productivity changes without formal training', in L. Lynch (ed) *Training and the Private Sector: International Comparisons*. NBER Comparative Labour Market Series. Chicago: Chicago University Press.

Weiss, R. (1993) 'Innovative trends in the field of in-company training' cited in K. Drake, The economics of learning on-the-job. A European perspective on instruction-led and experience-led job competence. Paper for conference on Efficiency and Equity in Education Policy, Canberra, 1995.

Woodhall, M. (1997) 'Human capital concepts' in A. Halsey, H. Lauder, P. Brown and A. Wells (eds) *Education, Culture, Economy, Society*. Oxford: Oxford University Press.

Zarifian, P. (1991) cited in Onstenk, J. (1997) Innovation, work teams and learning on-the-job. Paper for the EU Seminar Knowledge and Work, Amsterdam.

Zemke, R. (1985) 'The Honeywell studies: how managers learn to manage', *Training* August: 50-51.

Zey, M. (1984) *The Mentor Connection*. Homewood, Illinois: Dow Jones Irwin.

Zuboff, S. (1988) *In the Age of the Smart Machine*. New York: Basic Books.